Early praise for *Perfect Practice*…

"Our life comes under the control of one or the other—presence in love or escape in fear. *Perfect Practice* offers us hope by defining the wisdom that pain offers. This wisdom brings with it freedom from our own fearful thoughts. I have been entranced by the many interesting stories, lessons and gems of wisdom scattered throughout this book. I believe you, the reader, will too."

—KEN KORNELIS, PHD, Psychologist

"This book is one woman's journey, and I find it to be profound."

—CAROLYN HUNT, Legacy of Legends

"Every now and then, a book comes into your life at just the right time. This has been one of those books for me, and I know it will be that way for many of your readers. Thank you for sharing your life on these pages."

—JENNIFER ZACZEK, Founder, Cypress Editing

"The imagery in this book is vivid and the ideas paradigm shifting. Once I began reading, it was hard to put down."

—KIM WELSH, Upward Rise

"As a coach, speaker, and writer, Mary Corning is a storyteller of the first rate. I invited her to speak with my team of corporate recruiters about the art of influencing others, and for ninety minutes she had them actively engaged in exploring concepts of speaking truth in uncomfortable situations. Through it all Mary demonstrated her exceptional sense of humor, listening skills, and ability to ask questions that go right to the heart of the matter. It was an inspiring team meeting—one of our best!"

—CLAUDIA FAUST, Director of Talent Acquisition
Providence St. Joseph Health

PERFECT PRACTICE

A Philosophy for Living an
Authentic and Transparent Life

~

MARY S. CORNING

**CIRCLE
AROUND**
PUBLISHING
NEWBERG, OREGON

Circle Around Publishing
P.O. Box 275
Newberg, OR 97132
www.CircleAroundPublishing.com
www.MaryCorning.com

ISBN: 978-1-7329938-0-8 soft cover
ISBN: 978-1-7329938-1-5 special edition
ISBN: 978-1-7329938-2-2 ebook

Cover design: Olivia Croom, Indigo: Editing, Design, and More
Interior design: Vinnie Kinsella, Indigo: Editing, Design, and More
Cover photo: Mary Corning
Author photo: Magnus Bergroth

The quotes by Ray Hunt, Tom Dorrance and Joe Wolter are used with permissions.

The quote by Stephen and Ondrea Levine on p. 170 is from Stephen and Ondrea Levine, *Embracing the Beloved: Relationship as a Path of Awakening* (New York: Anchor Books, 1996), p. 255.

Publisher's Cataloging-In-Publication Data
(Prepared by The Donohue Group, Inc.)

Names: Corning, Mary S., author.
Title: Perfect practice : a philosophy for living an authentic and transparent life / Mary S. Corning.
Description: Newberg, Oregon : Circle Around Publishing, [2019]
Identifiers: ISBN 9781732993808 (softcover) | ISBN 9781732993822 (ebook)
Subjects: LCSH: Conduct of life. | Authenticity (Philosophy) | Self-actualization (Psychology) | Attitude (Psychology) | Change (Psychology)
Classification: LCC BF637.C5 C67 2019 (print) | LCC BF637.C5 (ebook) | DDC 158.1--dc23

Printed in the United States of America

Dedication

It is with a full heart that I dedicate *Perfect Practice*
to those who guided me along the way. These are the
master teachers who offered the sacred gift of wisdom.
Ray Hunt
Tom Dorrance
Joe Wolter

~

And most of all
to the horse.
I am still listening.

"I'll never be perfect, but I won't settle for anything less."

—Ray Hunt

Contents

Introduction

I AM A STUDENT OF THE SOUL. THROUGHOUT MY LIFE I have searched for and found master teachers who have led me in pursuit of a perfect practice. Perfect practice is not an act of perfectionism. It is a philosophy of not settling for less than perfect. Freedom is the ultimate reward. I realized that true freedom came from following my heart. This was not a solitary journey. I needed guides along the way. And as my philosophy dictated, I would not settle for just anyone to lead me. I became determined to learn from the masters of my craft, and my craft is a life well lived. As I began to understand the value of this profound journey, I also found the value of sharing it with others. This is the purpose of this book.

All my life horses have symbolized freedom. In my youth I did not question why I felt this way; I simply felt it in my heart. I loved horses long before laying hands on one. Even though I lived in the suburbs, I dreamed of riding in the mountains on these mystical, magical creatures that I adored from afar. I even spent several months of my allowance on an annual membership to save the wild mustangs. I read the newsletter that came with the wild horse subscription over and over and even recruited other kids to join. Finally my mother fulfilled her little girl's dream by booking a summer vacation at a ranch in central Oregon. That summer my bond with horses was forever set in stone.

My first ride on a horse was everything I had dreamed of. It was down a dusty trail, meandering through tall ponderosa pines. We crossed blue-water streams and then rode up steep hills, zigzagging high up Black Butte. The dark silhouette of this shadowy mountain offered a strong contrast to the snowcapped peaks that surrounded it. My future seemed to stretch out before me that day. My young heart was stirred. I found magic in the heart of the mountain, and most of all in the connection with the horse. I couldn't have known it then, but somehow I sensed my future forming. Like the trail I was following, I had no idea what was around the next bend. My entire life's purpose was set before I even knew what "a purpose" meant. To this day, when I crest a summit in the Cascade Range and see Black Butte's silhouette, I gasp in awestruck reverence. I formed a kinship with the mountain and the horse that summer. This was a lasting bond that had no end, only countless beginnings. This connection held my inner truth and set my path ablaze.

As I grew and began making choices on my own, I never lost sight of my childhood dream. The horse remained my guiding light and led me home again. In my early twenties I finally purchased my first horse. As fate would have it, this investment led me straight to the people who would offer the guidance I needed. I was riding blindly with passion and sought direction for my path. This path was to be my calling, and I was set to listen.

I lived a lot of life following this quest. I learned early on to never settle for less than what my heart beckoned me to do. If I were to succeed, I needed a teacher who taught with heart. The horse was there to carry me forward. I trusted I was on the right path. I was divinely led to the man who fit the bill perfectly.

There he stood in a dusty corral, stating with intensity he was there for the horse. Ray Hunt spoke his truth without wavering. He vowed never to settle for less than perfect practice. In a dirty felt hat, with a toothpick lodged between his teeth, he had a grin that captivated my inspired heart. Ray's voice commanded respect, and he received it. The students who met him would not forget him. I felt drawn to Ray in much the same way that I had been drawn to the horse and the mountain many years earlier. Ray was larger than life to me, and I knew he held the key. I was home again.

I gained much more than horse sense with my exposure to Ray Hunt. I gained insights to life. Life is what brought me to Ray, and life is what I was there to learn. The horse represented freedom in life, but I needed Ray to educate me as to how to utilize what I was beginning to recognize. I wanted to understand how to implement what I was learning—how to live it, not just learn it. It was not enough to simply buy a horse; I also had to learn to have a relationship with my horse. Horsemanship with Ray Hunt taught me how to resolve conflict, how to communicate requests, and how to understand what was effective and what wasn't. I had to become a good listener, a good student, and a good teacher. There it was—my education in real life. I never found it in a classroom with chalkboards and No. 2 pencils. I found it in a dusty corral, where leather chaps and saddles were the attire and grit and guts the prerequisites. This class in life could only be led by someone who lived it.

Ray Hunt was also a student who had looked for another way. He had come to a crossroads and sought a guide of his own choosing. Ray found his teacher in Tom Dorrance. Ray found a new way with horses in what Tom knew to be truth. Tom possessed a gift of awareness and compassion not only with horses but also with all life. It was simply and poetically part of who he was as a man. He understood the horse as a living, thinking, and spiritual being. The horse was not just a tool but also a friend and a partner. Tom held horses in high regard. This knowing that Tom possessed stirred in Ray a longing for learning. The ideal trilogy of student, teacher, and horse offered within it a hidden curriculum for a much deeper wisdom. This was not a how-to, dogmatic curriculum. It was a philosophy about life.

There is wisdom to gain in the philosophy of working with horses. I recognized that the same wisdom also applied to life. I saw that horses and life were equally responsive to this positive shift I was making in myself. As my approach to life changed along with my approach to horses, I felt more confident and clear in my intentions. The philosophy I was learning offered a deeper understanding of what I really wanted out of life. The freedom I had chased as a child was now within reach. Blending the study of horses and the study of life created a lasting change in me. I was finally able to bring into practice what I had felt in my heart all along.

Over the years, I have grown and learned with my horses. Now I enjoy the opportunity to share with others what I have learned. I don't see what I do (or what others do, for that matter) in terms of right or wrong. I can, however, see clearly when things are effective or ineffective. I am happy to share what has proven to be effective in my life and with my horses. I also understand that what I do may not fit everyone.

My teachers openly stated that if they were offering an example (at a clinic) and that example didn't fit when we got back home, it was best to reconsider. We needed to take responsibility and notice what was effective in any given situation. They encouraged us not to become dependent on the teachings but to let the teachings guide our inquiry. This would allow us and our horses the flexibility of learning. There is no one answer to fit all situations.

The messages, memories, and stories offered here are meant to present concepts to ponder. These are philosophies that (I hope) will open new ways of seeing things. Folks may have their own way of interpreting these ideas. The interpretation can easily shift the meaning for any individual. As I quote these great teachers, I wish to state that I am sharing my interpretations of the teachings. This is extremely important to keep in mind. My interpretation of Tom's and Ray's messages has been filtered through my individual life experience.

Throughout my work with people, I have heard the question, "What do I do?" Typically there is only one person who can accurately answer that question, and that is the person asking it. Each day and each life are variables. My suggestions are not meant to be taken as fact but rather as concepts to explore. This is why I tell stories. Stories set up visualization. I hope that by reading the stories, you will have a chance to feel as well as think about them. I hope to relate these ideas not only intellectually but also emotionally and spiritually.

Relating to the concepts is how I learned from Ray and Tom. Long after being at a clinic, I would relate an idea that I heard there to something I was seeing at home in my horse. I rarely knew exactly what it was that I was learning at each clinic. The learning came long after the clinic ended. I looked forward to unpacking the messages not all at once but in pieces here and there along the way.

This book is meant as a seed. I hope its message offers inspiration for living an authentic and transparent life. I intend for my personal stories to act as a true example of what can be gained when we follow our hearts. The willingness to meet life on life's terms is what opened me to understand my purpose and my process. When I understand life (and horses) on a deeper level, I begin to let go of the need to control every little detail. Life ceases to feel so heavy and cumbersome when we simply allow it to be. Without the dependency of control, I am open to experiment. The freedom of experimenting and observing has offered me lasting success. I learn not only a way of fixing but also, more importantly, a way of living. This process has formed a positive cycle for both me and my horses. Perfect practice is just that — it is a process. We don't become proficient all at once. We gain insight along the way. I hope by sharing some examples of my life, my words will inspire you to look outside the box. After all, life is an exploration. It is a remarkable journey into oneself when we seek first to understand. In doing so we find our compassionate heart.

CHAPTER ONE

A Good Start: Peaceful Presence

T HE MORNING AIR SMELLS OF FRESH RAIN. IT IS DAMP and chilly. I contemplate having a fire outside to sit by and write. This is springtime in Oregon. After the long winter I am tempted by any opportunity to hear the sound of morning birds. So I settle for frosty fingers to hold my morning tea. I stand wrapped in my Pendleton wool blanket, breathe in the cold, rain-soaked air, and notice my herd of horses cresting the hill. One by one they become acutely aware of an un-identified presence behind them. Something has alerted them. The bone-rattling sound of my dog's territorial bark assures me it must have been a coyote. This is a common morning ritual. The coyotes on their rounds innocently trigger the alarm. This heightened sensory perception can be viscerally felt. I, too, jolt as blood runs quickly through my veins, rapidly stirring my sleepy, contemplative morning mind.

I am guessing it wasn't a specific thought running through the horses' minds that turned them away from their habitu-ated path. It was simply keen awareness that stopped them in their tracks. They stand erect—listening, sensing, smelling, and waiting. They stand tall and ready, squarely and firmly present in the moment. For this moment, prior to reaction, they were perfectly still. I watch.

Defense is easy for me to identify physically in both horses and humans. Horses on high alert sound the warning call by trumpeting air through their nostrils and running full throttle for safety. With their hooves pounding the ground, I sometimes feel them coming before I see them. Here by the house is their barn, their home base and the center of their universe. There is no individual when the herd runs for survival. The herd is one. They move like a flock of birds in the sky, all shifting direction, slowing or speeding together as if they had radio signals. Today's alarm was benign. The heightened state of alert awareness soon diminishes. They return to peaceful morning grazing and I to my writing.

We experience presence rising up from behind the barrier of thought in times of emotional intensity. Not only in responses for survival but also in times of wonder and awe. The wonder in seeing the innocence of a newborn fawn or a beautiful sunrise peeking through the fog in the dense forest momentarily stops us in our tracks. We, in a sense, forget to think. It is like hitting the pause button in our mind.

We experience presence rising up from behind the barrier of thought in times of emotional intensity.

Heightened awareness can also be felt when circumstances take the mind by surprise, such as when we hear shocking news or experience a frightening close call. We can recognize presence when the mind (or our thoughts) can't quite catch up with what is happening in the moment. I felt this intensely when I received a phone call that my mother had suddenly passed away. It was shocking news. I couldn't think, but there was an awareness that led me through those first hours. This feeling is sometimes called surreal. But actually it is much more real than thought because the presence I feel is changeless and timeless. It is unconditioned. I have experienced this alert awareness in the depth of grief as well as in joyful exhilaration.

It's easy for us humans to become immersed in thought. Too many thoughts of right and wrong, success and failure, and enough or not enough create a constant dialogue in the mind—a dialogue of duality. This inner conflict can intercept the clear intention of the heart. I see the heart as an essential element for peaceful presence. While alert presence in the horses comes from a natural survival response, I suggest that humans, too, hear the survival call asking us to return to presence. Ours, however, is a different kind of survival; ours is survival of the heart.

I sense the call of survival in my heart through my natural desire for peace. Like the horses, my preference for peace initiates alert awareness. The paradox of my process is that my call for peace often comes in the form of conflict in my life. Contrasting circumstances such as joy and sorrow, health and illness, or abundance and scarcity act as gauges that I have learned to read. My experiences can tell me if I am living effectively from my heart or fearfully from my thoughts. I know what feels good and what does not. The real key has been to identify and understand the cause of the contrast.

I can also help my horse resolve resistance when I understand what is causing him to react. Horses give signals when they feel resistance just like humans do. A swishing of the tail and pinning of the ears are early signs. If I don't recognize the signs, they can easily become more dramatic. Unattended resistance can lead to more serious problems. It's not enough that I know what the signs mean. To be successful, I must also understand their cause. What are the signals pointing to? When I know the cause, I can more easily find the cure. There are signals in life telling me I need to become aware—to listen and to understand.

When I learn to read the signals, I can see that my reactions have great purpose. They alert me that I am defensive and troubled or peaceful and happy. They point me in the direction of my heart. My responses to life indicate where I am on my path. My thoughts and reactions can be my compass. Therefore, it is not (necessarily) my thoughts that bring me lasting peace. It is my presence. Alert awareness reminds me to stop and listen intently. Listen to what my body is telling me. Listen to my emotions and listen to my spirit. I can be still and let the keen and perfect awareness guide my thoughts. Once I recognized that this perfect presence existed within me, it became progressively easier to utilize. But first I had to become aware of it.

Watching the herd is an opportunity that helps me learn about awareness. I learn about the horses, but I also learn about my own natural defenses and reactions. Consistent observation is how I come to know myself and my horses better. I utilize the observations to educate myself about life. Observing the herd, I notice how they move. What is the first thing they do when they're frightened? What are the differences among the herd members? Is one more secure than another? I can clearly see each one's tendencies, and this makes me more prepared as a rider.

I realized the benefits of observation from the teachings of Tom Dorrance. Tom encouraged observation. He told of his early childhood in Wallowa County, Oregon, where he spent much of his time observing horses. He also mentioned observing people. Tom seemed to have found the value of observation early in his life. I understand now how observation can be a great benefit to expanding understanding for many things. Tom also encouraged us to remember what we notice and compare it to other things that we see when he said, "Observe, remember, and compare." I realized that observation is an important start, but we also need to understand what we are observing. As I look at my beautiful and diverse herd of horses, I see there is a distinct difference to each one of them. I stay aware from day to day and watch what things change and how they change. I keep track and make mental notes of the characteristics that I see. This helps me know my horses better. Observation has become an important part of my study of horses and of life.

I have learned to consciously rise above my habitual thoughts when I observe life without labeling it. Thoughts like *I'm too busy, there's never enough time* or *It's never going to stop raining* are statements that just aren't true, and they keep me stuck in a dialogue of wishing things were different than they are. When I notice myself making these statements, I can simply ask, *Is that so?* This simple question reminds me to free up my mind. As I become more aware of my habitual thoughts and inner dialogue, I diminish my dependency on them.

Habits form from an unconscious tendency. Consciousness defuses my habitual thoughts. I don't necessarily change thoughts. I live from the awareness of them. You might say I realize I am not my thoughts. This awareness offers freedom from thought addiction. I also experience this kind of freedom in meditation. A practice of quieting the mind is very important to allow presence to rise up from behind the habitual thoughts. Meditation doesn't have to be sitting in stillness. One of my ideal ways to meditate is simply listening deeply (or letting go of thoughts) while riding my horse in the forest. These are the moments when letting go of thoughts seems to suspend time. And in a sense it does, because timelessness is a very real attribute of presence.

Just like my horses when they stand perfectly still and focused, I, too, practice the art of listening. And I don't have to wait to be alarmed to do it. To the contrary, there are moments during my everyday life when I stop what I am doing (or thinking) to listen for the sheer pleasure of it, such as when I hear a

pair of red-tailed hawks circling high above me in the sky. They
dive and call to each other as if playing tag in the wind. The
sound of their freedom call is sometimes so faint I barely hear
it, and their silhouettes are only black spots against the white
clouds. But I'll clear all other sounds to listen. Even if a tractor
is running in the neighboring field, I will block the sound to hear
the hawks' calls. This deep attention is one way that I practice
detaching from the chattering thoughts of my mind and from
the busyness of the world.

Alert and perfect presence does not stem from the mind; it
comes from the heart. It resides deep in the center of us, behind
thoughts and judgments. There within this perfect, peaceful
presence resides our love for life, our appreciation of nature, and
our unconditioned connection to one another. If we feel we are
lacking these things in life, it is most likely the thoughts that
have stepped in the way of recognizing them.

Consistency of Awareness

Perfect presence is accessible to everyone, and perfect practice
draws sustenance from its depth. Our awareness of life is em-
bodied in presence. My awareness is always perfect. It is my
judgment that can be flawed. It is also my judgment that sees
things by contrast. Contrasting involves a positive and a negative side. Awareness is neutral. I have found that to work from
a success to a success is what's most effective in my life. It is not
only effective but also fun—it feels good! I am more peaceful
when I allow my thinking to be secondary rather than primary.
When I am conscious, I observe my thoughts from a state of
grace. This grace is an excellent place from which to live.

I am not proposing that we stop thinking, just that we let
go of our dependency on it. In a world of details and doings,

we often hurry past this peaceful foundation to implement our thoughts. This seems to me to be putting the cart before the horse. Awareness is consistent. When I allow awareness to lead me, I remain open to more options. My thoughts play an important supporting role, yet I am led by the positive influence of my open, abundant awareness.

Perfect practice is my ultimate ambition. I've seen the glimmering glimpse of the message of perfection, woven as a golden thread throughout a tapestry of philosophical traditions. The message that we may be free from suffering has been offered by master teachers from all walks of life throughout history. To ultimately achieve perfect practice would mean there is no more suffering, illness, sadness, or grief, because within perfection is nothing less than perfect. But of course this is the ultimate challenge.

When I first saw Ray Hunt work with horses, I recognized the same golden thread of aiming for mastery in perfect practice. At that time Ray had been well established as somewhat of a prodigy in the horse community. But like so many master teachers, he was not yet widely accepted by some old-school thinkers. It would take many decades and the rest of Ray's life for him to fully penetrate the world of horses. Ray Hunt had come into his calling. And he was ceaseless in his passion for it. Ray offered a deeper philosophy that he had come to understand through his relationship with Tom Dorrance. He learned from Tom a different way of understanding and educating horses. This was not a method or a doctrine; it was a new way of seeing. Changing perceptions and long-held paradigms does not necessarily come easy to a world that relies on things being dogmatic.

The first day I saw Ray, I sensed I was witnessing excellence within his intentions. Ray just carried a quality about him. It is difficult to describe in words. It seemed perhaps my perception of him was based on how I felt when I was near him. Ray had a way of saying things that stayed with me. I call them "one-liners" or "Huntisms." He encouraged us all to reach for standards I didn't even know were options. He set the bar high, and I have been reaching ever since. The premise for this book was born from Ray's quote "I'll never be perfect, but I won't settle for anything less."

I love that Ray was not willing to settle for less than perfection. I completely relate to that. I feel inspired every day by the opportunity to learn. Horses and life are both consistent and brilliant teachers. Observation (or awareness) is my curriculum. I could see that Ray saw beyond the obvious. He looked deeply into the horse. I saw that he could see the heart of the horse behind the horse's actions. I interpreted that he (and Tom) saw the good in the horse. This was exciting to me. I couldn't get enough of it. The good in the horse is perfect presence.

At the time I met Ray, I was chock-full of resistance. I was simply surviving in the world. I wasn't enjoying the ride. I had no idea of the influential power of presence or intentions. I only knew them on an intellectual level. I hadn't paid attention to how they could affect my life. I knew that I was drawn to the animals and to something beyond my thoughts and reactions. I was drawn to nonresistance and peace. But I could not identify that "presence" was what I was in search of. I had not yet identified the source of my problems. It seemed I was standing in the flames, holding the torch.

I knew that I wanted a feeling of peace. But I was still of the mind-set that I had to fight to get it. This was confusing and disorienting and just seemed to be getting me into deeper trouble. I felt like those scared horses looked. Somehow I realized that what I was thinking I "had to do" was not aligned with who I really was. I had learned these things from a harsh environment.

I related to those horses that were scared and threatened by their surroundings. I understood the horses' need for survival.

I knew that I wanted a feeling of peace. But I was still of the mind-set that I had to fight to get it.

I have come to realize that the horses people don't get along with are indeed the sensitive ones. The sensitive horses are the ones that won't quit you. They are the leaders, the survivors, and the best in the herd. Ray conveyed that the resistance or conflict in horses was most often presented to them by the human. The horse didn't ask to come into our world. The conflict came from us. I felt I identified with Ray's description of these horses. It was as if, in a very nondirect way, he was also speaking about me.

The Value of Forgiveness

Ray and Tom showed us that we could work through conflicts when we seek to understand the horse. Ray insisted it was our responsibility. Ray also taught us that no one sets out to be wrong, but when we realize our mistakes, we can go back and make things right. I learned about forgiveness. And I could see through Ray's example that making mistakes can even make us better. By learning to forgive myself, I was free to grow and learn. This freedom set me on a path that became a quest. I have not ventured from that path in nearly thirty years. It is the most gratifying thing you can imagine.

The horse was just trying to survive, and so was I. And so were all the people around me. Ray saw the horse as a horse — not as good or bad. Through this, I saw myself for the first time. Ray set the bar high for me. I began to understand there was free-dom in not settling for less than perfect practice. Perfect wasn't based on trying to be good. Perfect was based on the willingness to learn and the forgiveness of the need for survival. Realizing this, I, too, was no longer willing to settle for less than perfect.

Never settling for less does not mean chastising myself for being where I am today. It is much more about celebrating who I am and feeling excited about how I will grow into tomor-row. The ability (and inspiration) to observe and learn is how I evolve. Evolution is the energy of life—the motion of expansion. Advancement is not just for "those other people." I am growing every moment. We all are—whether we recognize it or not.

The essence of life (or the soul, if you will) reaches for har-mony. The mind needs contrast to label all that it sees. Contrast can also mean conflict. Therefore, if we rely solely on our thoughts in life, we will experience many great conflicts. This is not necessarily a bad thing as long as we have the whole picture in mind. I have come to use conflict as a good reminder to open my mind and essentially return to the path of peace. By doing this I make a potentially negative experience into a positive one.

This peaceful path is not necessarily an easy one to follow. In ancient scripture the entrance point was labeled "the narrow gate." When the gate is narrow, it's not always recognizable. I lose sight of it. Just like in my herd of horses, fear can engage my thoughts of escape. I may be sleepily dozing along in life, lost in the habits of the day-to-day, and forget who I am. Like the horses reacting to the coyote, I, too, can become alarmed and reactive. These are the times when perfect practice really pays off. When I am in practice of relying on awareness, it is much easier to resume my peaceful presence. I need only remember I have a choice. Awareness, observation, and nonresistance create the channel for perfect practice.

I used to think that the path of least resistance meant there is no conflict, but that is not so. The narrow gate is my willingness to learn. And as I learn, I develop my capacity to understand conflict. I see defense and conflict differently now, because I see that they are part of my education. I believe that in difficulty there is opportunity. I have lived it, and that is exactly what I want to share within these pages.

As prey animals, the horses' main objective is peace. Horses and humans alike can find a lot of turbulence along the path to realizing a peaceful existence. For a horse, survival is day to day. I see it as I watch the herd. My horses are well cared for and nurtured. But even they have a natural fear when faced with something unfamiliar.

In the forest near my house, there is a path with a water crossing. Albeit a very narrow trickle of water, it is deep. At this crossing, the water has carved out a crevasse under the tree roots. When I look at it, even I am a bit shocked. I assume my horse doesn't have any preconceived notion of this place on the path, other than that it looks like a black hole and that means danger.

As we approach this stream, I feel his entire weight shift under me. The forward motion is abruptly stopped. It feels a little like throwing a car into park while moving. There is great contrast in these moments. One moment I am riding along singing my song, and the next my horse slams on the brakes. His ears go up and his nostrils flare. I feel his whole body shift into reverse. I feel him preparing his mind and his body to turn around and head for home.

In the old days, before I began to grasp what Ray and Tom were sharing with me, I might have just reacted to my horse's resistance to cross the stream. I might have insisted he step over that spot even if he wasn't ready. This would have been like pushing him into the deep end before he could swim. I learned from Ray that we can get a horse ready or help prepare him for challenges, but there comes a time when you have to let him do his part. I have found that they will indeed do it when they are ready.

As I help my horse settle and pause, he becomes present rather than reactive. He looks, listens, and questions. And then finally, without force, he steps across. This not only gets us down the trail but also builds on our bond of trust. What could be more important than that? I now know the true value in the process. It is not about getting down the trail; it is about getting with my horse. And life is not about being right, successful, or approved of; it is about being present and finding the lesson in the conflict.

Fear-based thinking results from vulnerability of the body. Before I understood the process of perfect practice, my responses came from my instinct for survival. This was an extremely limited perspective. I found myself living life from a defensive posture, much like my horse would have if I had forced him across the stream. I was forcing myself to live without understanding the process.

Defensive posture includes ideas of protection, vulnerability, and sacrifice. These models were taught to me and for many years ruled my thoughts about life. They stemmed from what I call the "illogical logicals." These are the traits of the body. The biological can be the rush of adrenaline that sparks us to raise our voice or storm out in a conflict. The sociological may be prompted by our peers, families, or communities when they encourage us to believe we have a right to fight. And the psychological could show as the habits and perceptions that we picked up in childhood—all that we absorbed from our experiences long before we could intellectualize what it was we were learning. By itself, each of my human characteristics is a useful tool with a perfect purpose. The "logicals" only become "illogical" when I mistake them for who I am rather than a tool for my success. When I believe I am my thoughts, labels, and perceptions, it is like seeing the clouds and believing they are the sky. The sky holds the clouds. My thoughts are passing forms that move before my peaceful presence. I felt a peaceful presence in the teachings of Ray Hunt and Tom Dorrance. This I identified as the kindled fire in my heart—my life's purpose.

Now, decades later as I ponder Tom's words "Observe, remember, and compare," I realize the power of observation and the usefulness of understanding. I see things that I had frequently missed in the past. What I notice now has always been right before my eyes. I just wasn't aware of it. I feel as if layer by layer I am uncovering my vision. My sight was blurred by trying to achieve outcomes rather than seeing what was real in the moment. It was as if I was looking at my horse through a filter. Or worse yet, sometimes I didn't see the horse at all. I was simply seeing what I wanted him to be. It seems that now I do so much less and see so much more. I am letting go of controlling every little thing. This is a lifestyle for freedom. At last I am free to see life (and the horse) for what it is.

As I began to recognize my true nature, I also shifted the way I saw conflict. I started to use conflict as the tool for which it was intended. I could use my battles from the past as hindsight. I saw the patterns of fear in my historic conflicts. If I left a situation (or a horse) in fear, there was always a good chance that fear would remain intact. I soon began to realize that if I wanted something good, I had better pay close attention to how I left it.

This kind of fear patterning can happen behind the current scenes in our mind. On any given day, here where I live, if I hear a chain saw or bulldozer in the distance, I instantly tense up. I have a strong reaction that has nothing to do with what is actually happening in the moment. I acquired this reaction through a past experience.

I have always loved the forest. It is where I spent my time as a child. The trees, ferns, and wildlife served as my day care. The woods were my playground and my refuge. As an adult, I still seek solace and sanctity in the forest. I chose my twenty acres of land because it was located in the middle of a nine-hundred-acre wood. I felt at home.

I loved living in "the canyon," in the middle of the woods. But one day (several years after I moved in), I came home and heard a terrible sound. The sound was coming from a huge logging machine. It was heading straight toward the house, clearing every tree in its path. It cut, fell, and limbed each tree like a paper shredder. The sound was deafening and frightening. I instantly thought of all the animal lives being taken down along with all the beautiful trees. Thoughts of fear and survival filled my mind, and I was helpless.

This forestland next to my house held great value in my life and in the lives of so many. There were deer and elk, gray squirrels, and hawks that all shared this space with me. I had been the steward of this land for many years. The owners lived out of state, and they had asked me to keep an eye on it for them. I spent countless hours riding the trails and old logging roads, where deep, shade-covered paths were covered in clover and wildflowers. I galloped my horses up the steep hills and enjoyed the wind and the view at the top.

I had three horses at the time and shared enchanting experiences with each of them. My youngest horse, Far Go, was just a colt, and we would ride into the canyon where the blackberries were warmed by the sun. He loved the purple flower tops of the thistles that grew in front of the blackberry patch. Far Go held in his mind the memory of this place, and this memory offered great initiative to go into the woods. He knew there was a sweet treat at the end of the trail. We would trot down the trails as if on a mission and park next to the patch. I would have warmed blackberries for breakfast while he enjoyed carefully pulling the blossoms off the thistles without being poked. As I saw the huge machine mowing this forest, I felt it mow right over this treasured land in my heart.

I will never forget the sound and sight of the gigantic saw eating up the vast forest in its path. It took nearly a year, and they took almost all the trees on two hundred acres, right up to my fence line. Then they erected a six-foot cyclone fence and put in a vineyard. I pack this pain from my past. I unconsciously developed a hidden fear of the sounds I associated with watching the forest fall, and this fear distorts the perception of what I experience today.

Looking at it from a broader perspective, I could completely understand and empathize with the fear from this event in my past. I saw how it was created. But I also realized a strong desire to be free from this mournful fear. After the trauma of watching the trees fall, I thought freedom could only be achieved by moving away from the canyon. I began a search for a new place to live and a new forest to live in. While living deep in the woods remained a strong desire, I also realized running from my inner turmoil would not offer freedom. I had to come to terms with life on life's terms. I wanted clarity in my mind before I could move anywhere in peace. I began to recognize how out of place my reactions were to the sounds of vineyard machinery or a chain saw running in the nearby woods. It became vitally important to my well-being to focus and stay present in the moment. I had to stay very conscious that I did not increase the discomfort I experienced by bringing in my past. This became a consistent practice. Now I see how fear operates unconsciously in many areas of my life. Without awareness, fear becomes a silent partner. Unconscious fear challenges what is real. It gets in the way of peaceful presence and distracts me from perfect practice.

I grieved the loss of the forest. Grief is a conflict between what we want and what is. This conflict created pain, and my suffering came from resisting the pain (and the circumstances) it created. I had to learn to be compassionately aware of my pain. It wasn't enough to just ride through it and try to get over it. I had to understand it. I allowed myself to grow through the pain rather than simply go through it. This meant feeling all the emotions that came through me. There was anger, sadness, loss, and helplessness. Some of the grief lingers still. I took action where appropriate and let go in areas I could not change. I allowed my true nature to be felt and the past to be healed. This took time. Going through each part of the pain consciously meant I didn't get stuck in the unconscious pattern of defense.

Grief is a conflict between what we want and what is.

Holding true to the teachings of those whom I admire, I remember the premise—I may not be fearless, but I won't settle for less. When I am aware of what holds me back, my divine nature has a chance to support my growth and free me from unconscious resistance. Of course there is still conscious resistance, but we will address that later in the book. My first essential step in developing a policy of perfect practice is to simply be willing to see clearly, without the veil of fear. I seek to understand my feelings in order to release the clouded vision of the past.

When I am conscious, I can mindfully begin to heal the fear and let go—in love. Letting go in love frees up our future.

Resolving conflict is not about changing the past. It is about utilizing the present. Resolution doesn't come from leaving an experience in fear. The experience requires my understanding, even if understanding simply means being aware of the pain that I feel. Forgiveness comes from understanding. Forgiveness is how I release my painful past, remove the veil of fear, and clear the way for the next good start.

CHAPTER TWO

Tying the Ends Together

THE ART OF OBSERVATION IS AN INTOXICATING PAS-time. I'm not referring to simply watching or seeing, but to deep, pensive observation—like stargazing on a high desert or watching tides roll in. Observation is soul food. I value my time in the early mornings, sitting in stillness at the dawn of each new day and simply observing. From the comfort of my cozy tea chair, I quietly reacquaint myself with the world outside. The chair is placed before a cathedral window. A wood beam reaches to the top of the vaulted ceiling, and a cross brace divides the triangular windows. The symbol of the cross is not lost on me, as it is the focal point of the room. The windows reflect light, and the changing scenery moves like a revolving stained glass. The images are new and fresh each day. No two days are alike.

The background scene is a grassy hill beyond the window. The color scheme shifts from mint green in spring to a burnt gold in summer. A simple passing cloud can be enough to change the hue. There is a nut tree that offers shade in the summer and supports a feeding station for birds. The birds change shifts around mid-October when the wintering flocks arrive from the north. In the fall the nut-bearing tree occupies the blue jays' attention, and the tapping sounds fill the room while they crack their harvest on the back porch. Things don't seem to stay the same in nature. Life is ever changing. Observing the nuances of change opens and expands my vision of my world. Opening my mind frees me from the trap of unconscious habit. Perfect practice does not have to be challenging. Daily practice can be deeply rewarding and soothe the hurried mind.

Deep observation breaks up patterns. It could easily be perceived that I sit in the same chair, at the same time, and drink the same tea. And that would be accurate, but only on the surface. There is much more going on below the superficial layer of our lives. I can feel happy or sad, tired or inspired. There are times I feel fit and complete and times I feel weakened and achy. It is no different with my horses. They wake up in the same pasture or stall (depending on the weather) and look for their breakfast at the same time each day. They often wander to the water tank at about the same time or all decide to rest in the warmth of the morning sun. On the surface there seems to be many set patterns, but deep inside each horse there is a very different feeling. My pastime of observing horses has taught me a lot about seeing the obvious but also recognizing when something more meaningful has been overlooked. For example, the hindquarters of the horse. Tom said in his book *True Unity*, "The rider needs to get to the point where he realizes how important the hind quarters are." It seems obvious that it would be important to be aware of the hind feet, but they are frequently ignored.

Often people's attention is focused on the front of the horse. I think this is because that is what we see before us when we ride. We rely on our eyes for our guidance. I felt that Ray and Tom wanted us to feel the whole horse under us, and this feel went deeper than the outside of the horse. They suggested we learn to feel the inside too—his emotions and thoughts. To do this we can't get stuck simply seeing what is physically out in front of us. I realized that my sight could easily become a crutch. To notice the hindquarters of the horse, I had to focus on what I felt, not just what I saw. I had to change my natural dependency on sight. To develop a deeper level of observation meant utilizing all my awareness.

As I observe my horses on a deeper level, I learn things that couldn't come from an instruction manual. Ray and Tom both encouraged us to let the horse teach us what we need to know. The art of observation is a great asset to understanding our horses. We can learn to notice if they are sick or well, tuned in or turned off, defensive or content. Just like people, everything the horse feels can rise to the surface when we observe them in order to understand them.

Defensive Posture

I started to notice how my horses stood. Now I observe them standing in the herd or, when they are just saddled, waiting to be ridden. I pay attention during the rides, at the beginning and at the end. I look for patterns of behavior to help guide me to understand how they feel. I began to notice that they frequently stood in what I came to label a defensive posture.

Keep in mind I am saying a defensive, not aggressive, posture. The back feet offer a great deal of power for the horse. From defense to flight, the hind feet are the driving force. I noticed that while standing still, my horses often stood with one hind leg back, and commonly it was the right one.

Most domestic horses are strong to one side, much like people who are right-handed or left-handed. I presumed part of the horse's tendency to stand this way was caused by the human's habitual interaction with the horse. The majority of gear that people use is buckled, tied, or cinched on the left side of the horse. So horses grow accustomed to the person on their left. As a prey animal, a horse is instinctively aware of his escape route. Since the human is most often on the left side, the horse may reserve his right side as the escape route. I have observed my horses consistently pushing off with the left hind foot when escaping to the right. The right hind foot is back and out of the way to open the escape route. The more I noticed this, the more I realized how often horses are preparing for escape.

I thought about how fear and defense are at the heart of the need to escape. This alerted me to recognize the emotions that my horses commonly experience. Even though all the horses here have a very peaceful and happy life, they still can have the habit of fear. Inspired by this insight, I set out to improve their experience. By contrast, I could also see that when the horse was at ease or at rest, the hind foot was most commonly cocked and relaxed. I began to experiment to see if I could intercept this habit and offer a different way. And I had just the horses to practice on.

Fear and defense are at the heart of the need to escape.

Ray often said, "It's the little things that mean a lot to the horse." Standing at ease was something I had taken for granted for many years. Once I caught on to how helpful this was, I was amazed. I decided to help encourage my horses to bring their right hind foot forward and stand at ease when we are together. This little thing helped my horses a lot.

I enjoy different ways of communicating with horses. I see it as a relationship, and I like them to have a say in our interactions. I like to see what choices they would make without me always influencing their decisions. Having this broader perspective, I can identify their needs sooner. I can do less and allow the horse to do his part. I learn to stay out of his way. I don't try to fix the horse. I understand him, and he does the fixing.

I have a round corral and an arena I use to allow my horses a broader sense of freedom—unencumbered by a halter or a rope. Ideally my goal is to blend the horse's ideas with mine. My best experiences are when my horse and I want the same things. It is truly remarkable what horses will do when given an opportunity. They enjoy learning and love accomplishment, and when this includes release and nonresistance, they fill in with a style only they can provide. Horses are incredibly intuitive.

Over the years I have made a practice of asking their opinions as often as I can. This doesn't mean I don't provide leadership. I ask horses into my world when I request them to wear a saddle and carry me. I am obliged to lead the way for them. But good leadership comes with compassion and understanding. Conflict arises when understanding is lost. So it is of benefit to us both when we can have a combined voice for mutual understanding.

My first experience with moving a hind foot to change the defensive posture came while working with Bubba. Bubba is a big, gray draft horse that boards here at our barn. He is by far the largest horse in the herd. He is also the most timid. In the past, his fear response was explosive. I could see that Bubba would really benefit from a positive, consistent change. I wanted to offer a way that he could let his guard down and relax a little—not take life so seriously. I wanted to show him he could feel more at ease. I also realized he could teach me a lot.

As horses go, Bubba is an extreme introvert. In the herd, he usually stands off by himself; he abhors trouble. I suppose that he keeps to himself because of his timid nature. As I became more aware of the habit of the defensive posture, I noticed this tendency seemed extreme in Bubba.

Bubba's right hind foot was not just held back; it would often be stretched way out behind him. I suppose that enabled the explosive launch that was required for his large mass to move in a hurry. This stretched-out way of standing looked uncomfortable. I would guess Bubba needs those big, pizza-sized feet to be squarely under him to support his weight.

Bubba is also a large thinker. He really takes things personally. He contemplates and ponders, mostly from a distance. His expressive black eyes are accented with bright white eyelashes. When he is focused and thinking, the brows above his eyes form little peaks like snowcapped mountains. Bubba's head is the size of my entire upper body. When we work together, his mind sometimes becomes so full that he lowers his large head all the way to the ground. He'll stand there with long, lingering, blinking eyelids, resting his lip in the sand. I am guessing all that thinking weighs heavy at times for Mr. Bubba. I was happy to show him a way to feel good and accomplished.

The key to asking the horse to move a foot is in the release. Horses are extremely sensitive, and they are seeking peace. Tom and Ray shared with us that they are searching for release from pressure. A big misconception in people who do not understand horses can be the use of force. Human beings are conditioned to use force. Force is the nature of a predator. But for a prey animal, life depends on running away from force. By their own divine nature, horses willingly yield (or relax) when pressure is released. Recognizing natural differences in our tendencies and reactions helps me build a deeper relationship with my horses. Perfecting the timing of my release is a fundamental aspect of what I strive for and a golden nugget of what I learned from watching Ray and Tom.

When there is a release of pressure, horses will remember, as Ray said, "what happened before what happened, happened."

They stay alive by accurately remembering what gave them release. Horses are masters at finding the path of least resistance. The unfortunate aspect of their interaction with people is that humans don't commonly think in terms of release. With this in mind, it is easy to see the conflict in the nature of the relationship between man and horse. All too often the horse's main focus is on escaping the pressure, while his human counterpart is pouring it on. Ray reminded us that we are the ones who introduce conflict to the horse. The horse doesn't want any part of conflict, yet he sometimes has no other choice but to push back.

The natural sensitivity in horses allows them to continue as a species. Bubba is chock-full of this sensitivity. As I observed from the middle of the round corral, Bubba moved freely around the rail and then stopped. True to his nature, he'd leave his right hind foot back. I understood that to move a foot he had to take his weight off it. All I really had to do for his weight to shift was make a small motion toward him. From this standpoint it was easy to see when he took his weight off his hind foot. The next logical thing to happen was that he would pick it up. I learned to shift his weight so I could move his feet. I heard Ray mention this time and again. Shifting the weight is what happens before what happens, happens. As soon as I saw the shift in his balance, I stopped, or sometimes I would even back up.

When I backed up I gave Bubba the release of pressure he wanted. And like a rubber band springing back after tension is released, his weight would shift back and forth. I was thinking about Ray's message to be particular rather than critical. I was careful to keep what I was doing with Bubba simple and consistent.

Bubba is a linear thinker. Once he became aware that I was offering consistency of release, he was more than happy to move the hind foot forward. With that kind of desire, it was fairly simple to carry this lesson into the saddle. In the saddle I have the opportunity to shift his weight and release at (or preferably just before) the point he picks up his hind foot. The element that took the longest for me to learn was feeling what was happening so that I could do my part for the release. I had to be able to feel the hind feet under me. The horse is a patient teacher when force is not involved. The ability for us to remain conscious was of great benefit to the process. Once I developed my timing, I could clear the way for Bubba to do his part. He was happy and more than willing to comply. Soon Bubba's habit was to stand at ease, and that was the beginning of shifting his habit of fear.

Ending any experience in a positive feeling is a great practice for success. This holds true with horses and in life. Basking in the feelings of unity and success opens not only our minds but also our hearts. I really enjoy pausing after a pleasurable ride on my horse. I soak in what is taking place between us. You might say I take a moment to appreciate our bond. This appreciation brings out the best in both of us. I have seen a lot of horses looking for a break from being asked to perform. These horses just can't wait for the rider to hurry and step down. I take lots of physical and mental breaks during my rides. I make it my practice that the last thing I do with my horse is simply nothing. I don't ask anything of him. This has become a favorite ritual. More times than not my horses will yawn or sigh and lick their lips in complete relaxation before I step down. At this point it seems they don't really mind if I get off or not; they feel good. They are soaking in their accomplishments. I learned from Ray to let the horse enjoy feeling accomplished. After all, they are the ones who are learning to do what we are asking of them. I want to give them the recognition they deserve for such a remarkable achievement. When I can do that, my horse enjoys being with me. I want that feeling to linger until the next time I saddle him and ride. Everyone benefits by leaving the experience with a peaceful presence.

The flip side is true as well. When I start my rides, I don't just get on and go. I check in and let them settle. I let them have some time to check in with me. I like them to be curious about what we might do today. Horses like learning; it stimulates their minds. But there is a big difference between being in a learning frame of mind and being forced to perform. Ray reminded us to treat horses as we would want to be treated.

I can empathize with how it feels to be asked to learn something that seems to have no meaning. I was the kid in school who asked, "Why?" I never understood the importance of learning certain subjects. I wanted to know the application. Many kids did what they were told simply because they had to. I didn't fit into that category, and this made for a lot of resistance in my childhood. I noticed early in life I didn't follow the crowd. This taught me to be independent but packed with it a whole lot of lonesomeness.

Being independent I learned the true value in my life. It has always been "my life," not someone else's opinion. With this tendency I also related to horses that questioned authority. Horses that people would call rogue or renegade, I called sensitive and passionate. These were the horses I would choose. I saw myself in each of them. I know that when I have a strong desire to learn something, I commit myself completely. This has also helped me see the true value of building desire in the horse.

When I ride my horse, I begin slowly. I let him warm up physically but especially mentally. I want to feel him from the inside out. The first step is as important as the last. I want both steps and all steps in between to be of quality. And now (as often as I can) I encourage the first step and the last to be a hind foot forward.

It seems so simple that it's difficult. Attention to the smallest things makes a big difference. Before we can have unity, we must undo the habit of fear. Fear is what precedes conflict. And understanding transcends fear. These seemingly simple tasks of paying attention and being patient to subtly help the horse let go of fear and resistance have led to transcending conflict. Everything I do with the horses has improved. Understanding and experimenting with the defensive posture showed me a lot about what I had been missing. I was able to increase the horse's desire to learn. Not necessarily because of what I did, but because changing the unconscious habit shifted how he felt. I was able to create a positive environment for learning. And this helped us (the horse and me) be successful and effective. The shift of the attention from what we do to how we do what we do has really made a difference in the relationship I have with my horses. We both tend to enjoy the ride. After all, life is too short not to.

Before we can have unity, we must undo the habit of fear. Fear is what precedes conflict. And understanding transcends fear.

Human relationships, too, can greatly improve and expand if each time we leave each other just a little better than when we met. This quality of not settling for less even applies to the most difficult of relationships. We need not settle for a painful past to create our future. We have the power to change how we respond to life and to all our experiences. We don't have to settle for feeling bad when feeling good could be just one simple, conscious step away.

Ray, Tom, and the horse have shown me how valuable awareness can be. In difficult conversations or anytime fear is present,

I can find a success. I can pause, take a breath, take a walk, or just close my eyes for a moment. As conscious human beings, we can be aware of defensive patterns. Unconscious habits can keep us living in a defensive state of mind. Sometimes these habits are as simple as a roll of the eyes or clench of the jaw. These are examples of our defensive posture. When we are conscious of what we do, we can intercept these actions and transition to something that feels good. A smile or a pause can change an entire interaction. This is the beginning of taking our lives back from the habituated mind and learning to work from a success to a success. This is one part of unlearning the habit of fear and defense, and in the process, we transcend conflict. We can practice "cocking a hind foot."

A Learning Frame of Mind

I wanted nothing more than to learn to be a good horsewoman. And I wanted to learn from these masterful teachers. For this to happen, I had to make a lot of changes in my life. My desire to learn was piqued, but I had to develop a learning frame of mind. In my childhood I associated education with pain. I never felt that I was good enough, so I just didn't try. I never felt the desire to learn. So I just survived. I see this (survival) in the eyes of horses too. I want to do for them what Ray did for me. I want to offer a reason for the horse to have a learning frame of mind. When I met Ray Hunt, a sudden rush came over me, and I wanted to know everything I could learn. I still have that burning desire today. That fiery spark has never weakened. I want to see that spark in my horse's eye.

Through horsemanship, I learn complex life lessons. I go deeper into myself. I experience open-minded willingness. I learn to accept mistakes. Having the desire to learn means that I seek to understand. This involves letting go of what I think I know. I see growth as a luxury rather than a hardship. All these characteristics have greatly improved my life. I am no longer simply surviving. I am enjoying life. Horses have given me the tools to evolve as a person. This is what I wanted to learn in school. I wanted to learn how to live. These are the life skills I value.

My consciousness is a gift that allows my mind to open. I tend to close my mind when experiencing fear or defense. I react rather than respond. I limit my options. Engaging in defense is practicing resistance. The word *react* denotes habit. Re-act, as in "to repeat." Reaction stems from an unconscious habit of doing. To offer a response is to think and feel from my consciousness. A conscious response offers me choices. Defense limits them.

I have experienced great conflicts while in defense. My reactions are not who I am. They are my unconscious habits. Fear reactions are about as effective as pulling on a lead rope when a horse is pulling back. The more a person pulls, the harder the horse pulls back. I've seen horses pull away and take off running, dragging the rope. Or if they are tied to (or with) something they can break, it's even worse. Pulling hard enough to break free can cause all kinds of problems down the line. It can be a difficult habit to overcome in a horse. When a horse has learned to pull with all his might for freedom, it is pretty hard to convince him otherwise. The next time he feels resistance, he may go right back to the same amount of pressure that got him a release the last time. Remember, horses know what happened just before what happened, happened. They don't forget the path to freedom.

I was this way growing up. The first time I ran away to the woods, I was in kindergarten. I continued this habit of finding my release through escape throughout my life. When I didn't like how things were going, I simply took myself out of them. I was good at being alone. So this meant I left many relationships

in the dust. This tendency finally turned around when I began
to understand it was a reactive habit, not an effective response.
Leaving as an empowered choice is one thing, but leaving in fear
is settling for and practicing what I don't want. Leaving in fear
meant I was sure to find it again. Fear was what I practiced, so
fear was what I lived.

Thankfully I learned early on that if a horse wants to pull, it
is best not to give him something to pull against. I found it is
much more effective to be in a position to help direct his energy.
I learned that this is the difference between being responsive
and being reactive. I began to see a parallel in my life when I
watched people ineffectively trying to control and discipline
a frightened horse. As I watched, I wondered what they were
thinking. Then I realized that's what I do in times of trouble.
I push back against life—against the things I can't change. I
realized that I was every bit as ineffective with my thoughts as
the person pulling on the rope. I decided to use my empathy
for horses to show me a different way to cope. Soon I found
that I could redirect my thoughts and be much more effective.
I could let go.

As far as I can tell, the misconception that resistance can
offer release is a fatal flaw. But it does provide a great contrast
to illustrate the importance of responding rather than reacting.
When I stay present and aware, I can still engage without developing a habit of resistance. This is what I refer to as "letting go
of the rope." When a rope is pulled tight and one end is released,
how much resistance is left in the rope? Resistance requires engagement. We can choose to disengage without departure. This
I have personally found to be effective.

In challenging situations I can respond rather than react.
This not only relieves the pressure but also allows me to learn
from the experience. It is my response-ability, or my ability to

respond. It takes practice to stay conscious in conflict. I have learned some wonderful ways of creating effective habits by letting go of the unconscious ones. One way I learned to be effective is to be early.

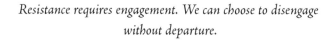

Resistance requires engagement. We can choose to disengage without departure.

Ray reminded us that it is much easier to be early and stay clear of trouble than it is to get out of it. I see that when I react rather than respond, I am late. When I am defensive, I have engaged. I am pulling on the rope. Being aware of my feelings and the reactions of others really improved my timing. I can see clearly that if a horse is pinning his ears or swishing his tail that he is experiencing some resistance. I wanted to learn to read life situations the same way. When I am early it's easier to recognize my own defensiveness and that of others.

I learned to become aware of the notorious "line in the sand." The point when things go from feeling good to feeling bad is variable. Because the line is in the sand, it can be moved. Confidence formed from the willingness to not settle for fear is how I move the line.

I can recognize those transitions in myself and in my horse. Ray shared the idea that good judgment can come from bad experience. I have had enough bad experience to build a wealth of good judgment. With horses and in life, if I miss those early warning signals, I can get hurt. But when I'm aware, coming from a learning frame of mind, I can respond rather than react. An early, mindful response to horses or to life can defuse a conflict. "Letting go of the rope" can turn what might be a painful situation into an opportunity for success. Ray taught me that to be effective with my horse it's best to help keep him on the outside edge of trouble. That doesn't mean we don't sometimes find out that there is trouble; it just means we don't go out and look for it. I see the same in life. There is trouble, and there is resistance, but I can find success when I can have an effective response.

Several years ago, a group of friends gathered at my place for a ride. It was a fresh spring day, and I convinced our group that we should ride up the road for an outing. The arena is a great place to practice certain skills and give the horses some confidence. But nothing beats heading out into the world to see what life might present to us.

The rhythm and power of a herd on the move is a sight to behold. The sound of six horses' hooves on a gravel road serenaded my soul. That crisp spring day, riding with friends, lifted my spirit and filled my heart. We rounded the corner at the end of the private road and entered the main road leading past farms and vineyards. From that point we could see all the way to the Coast Range mountains. The view is vast. It is wide open to both east and west.

Bordering the road we were riding was a large field fenced with old wire. I was on my horse Far Go, who takes his role of leadership very seriously. One vet I knew called him a type A personality. Suffice it to say that he doesn't miss a thing. The farther from home we rode, the wider the nostrils on the horses became. Their senses came alive; sight, smell, and sound all increased in sensitivity with the freshness of a new experience. When we approached the field, we noticed a llama sleeping about twenty yards away. As she stood to see the herd coming toward her, the horses saw her. Each one spun on its heels and turned tail to run. Just like that, we had our opportunity to learn.

The llama had no idea that, to our horses, she closely resembled a hairy walking boulder. She was curious and started to trot right toward the herd. The horses were having no part in this. They were not going to stay around and make a new acquaintance. There were snorts and blows, whirls and gasps. Each rider grabbing for the reins tried to manage and take control of the unique situation. Within a few minutes, everyone regained composure.

When we get far enough away from what frightens us, we start to relax and return to our senses. This can be true for horses as well. We moved the herd about one hundred yards down the road. As we all visited about what had happened, I suggested we use the experience to improve our connection with our horses. I might add that this suggestion was met with a bit of resistance. I assured my friends that no one would have to do anything that didn't feel right. No one would get left behind. Holding true to the benefit of the learning frame of mind, we have to work with people (and with horses) from where they are.

At a distance of one hundred yards, the riders and horses felt relatively secure. By riding Far Go toward the llama, I showed my friends a great visual reference of moving the line in the sand. As I rode Far Go away from the herd and toward what frightened him, his whole body began to tighten. I could feel—and the other riders could see—Far Go's degrees of transition from feeling good to feeling bad. Taking one step toward the llama was three on a scale from one to ten. But twenty feet away from the herd, Far Go quickly reached a nine.

As I circled around and returned to the herd, all the riders could see the changes in Far Go—from confident to fearful and back to confident again. Each rider had the advantage of witnessing this from a sense of security and a comfortable distance. There was no force to go beyond what they felt was their capacity for learning. This builds confidence and encourages a learning frame of mind in both horses and riders. We moved the line of fear incrementally and worked from a success to a success. Each time we returned to the herd, Far Go was reassured. He was not held against his will. Soon he actually became curious about the llama. This is a great shift in the mental process. Changing fear to curiosity is a powerful mental shift that can quickly transfer to the body, helping it relax.

Changing fear to curiosity is a powerful mental shift.

The horses were of the opinion that this llama was not natural to their environment. The alarm was real for them. They were not wrong for feeling the need to escape; this is their innate mode of survival. Of course as riders, we knew the llama was innocent, but there was no way to force a horse (or a person) to achieve peace from a state of fear. Allowing them to learn means that we show them compassion and patience.

After witnessing the success with Far Go, all the riders agreed to ride toward the llama. We would reassure and pet our horses even for the thought of willingness. If the horses felt the need to turn away, the riders could just go with them, acknowledging no horse was forced to stay where he didn't want to be. We could even trot a little way toward home. Then, as we circled around to look at the llama again, we would sit quietly and encourage the horse to feel that peaceful presence. Whenever the horses looked at the llama, we would be quietly supporting them.

The llama experience actually taught the horses they could relax. There were times we would turn toward home even before the horse had returned to a state of fear. Turning away would relieve the pressure while things still felt good, instilling again a feeling of success. The horses found that they had conquered their own primal response of fear and escape. And they did it through feeling peaceful! This is perfect practice, and it was a powerful lesson for both horse and rider.

Each time we headed toward the llama and circled back, we would move the line of comfort closer and closer to it. Soon we were about twenty yards from the llama. Even when the horses were approached by the llama and started to worry, it wouldn't affect them nearly as much. We directed their feet with ease and trotted away. Then we would trot a circle back to the point of departure (or even closer). Each time we moved the line a bit closer to the llama, we would stand at ease and rest. All of this took about fifteen minutes. Soon our courageous herd walked right past the llama, each horse licking his lips and blowing out the steam that fear had built. The horses felt uplifted and so did the riders.

We cease being victims of life and all its fears when we realize that contrasting emotions can teach peace. The contrast of peace and fear taught the horses (and the riders) that they could feel good even near the thing that scared them. The conflict actually created the opportunity to build confidence.

Perfect practice enables a shortcut in the long run. The next time the horses confronted what looked like a hairy moving boulder, they were curious and courageous. And even if there was a bit of fear, both horse and rider knew that they could find the direction for success.

We can all benefit greatly from a learning frame of mind. Life is not always about a peaceful ride down the road, with no bumps and "boos." We can learn to understand our fear and build confidence in ourselves and our horses. A learning frame of mind does not include force or coercion. If we had just spurred them forward, it would have looked like a barroom brawl. We can learn to dance in unity with our horses and with life's circumstances. A good start on perfect practice is remembering that we have the choice in every situation to stay present and develop our capacity for peace.

CHAPTER THREE

Releasing the Past

HORSES ARE FULL OF SURPRISES. PHRASES LIKE "WELL, you never know" and "I didn't see that one coming" become a big part of the common vocabulary. I heard both Tom and Ray speak about the beauty of acquiring skill and know-how—as part of the concept that it takes a lifetime to learn to live a lifetime. Experience can't be bought; it has to be acquired. But just because we live through something doesn't mean we have gained the wisdom from it. Sometimes it takes a whole lifetime of living to open ourselves to the lessons of life.

When I entered the world of horses, I had no previous experience. One might say I was "green as grass." *Green* is a term that is used for young colts that have little experience. I didn't grow up on a ranch; I grew up in the suburbs. My childhood was a bit troubled. I was the youngest of four children. My father moved away when I was five, and my mother went to work. I acted out in school and quickly became labeled a reckless child. My reckless tendency made me tough. But I was street tough, not cowboy tough. I learned about life by living at full throttle. I was the child who ran with scissors. I learned to hide my fear and mask it as resistance. That was until I found my heart's passion in living with horses. With horses, I finally conceded to my fear and was stripped of my resistance.

You just never know when you get up in the morning what that day will bring. It was a day like any other day that brought me to surrender. My horse Far Go was (at the time) a young colt with limited experience. I started him at a clinic and had followed up with some trail rides. He had been hauled in the trailer several times, but truthfully he was green as grass. The driveway leading to my home is steep. It would seem I have a propensity for living in canyons. I like the seclusion and shelter of the canyon walls. I built my place tucked in the middle of a forest. The nearest neighbor is a half mile away. My road is the road less traveled. I have always liked it that way. The liability in that is the limited options should I need help.

I had an appointment to bring Far Go to the vet for a simple dental exam. I hooked the trailer to the truck and loaded him with no problem. Just before I left, I ran into the house for a bottle of water. I heard a terrible crash and looked outside and saw the vent on top of the horse trailer shoot straight up in the air like a launched rocket. I ran out and looked inside the trailer. All I saw was Far Go lying flat on his back, all four feet sticking straight up in the air. Seeing his tongue hanging out, I thought he might have been dead.

I was all alone. In my young life I had never known anything similar to a feeling of hysteria, but that was exactly what I was feeling. Pure, raging emotion took over. All I felt was a shattering breakdown of my complete mental capacity. There was no one around to scream for, so I screamed to God for help. All I could do was pray.

The trailer was a two-horse straight-load trailer. Nowadays trailers are designed to be much more user-friendly, with horses hauling on a diagonal. But this was an old trailer with a manger in front where you tied the horse's head. Far Go had somehow gotten his front feet up in the manger and pushed back so hard in panic that he broke the snap on the rope. This sent him catapulting backward in the trailer. Far Go was wedged upside down in his stall.

I slowly opened the back door of the trailer, and his head dropped out. Just then he erupted with the force of one thousand pounds of pure self-preservation. All I could do was get out of the way. I buried my eyes in my arms; I couldn't bear to see what would come next. With a fury of fright and the crashing of metal, I heard a pause and peeked over my sleeve. He was high-centered over the bar dividing the stalls. I closed my eyes as the next round of chaos in the trailer started. Unimaginable fright sent blood rushing in my veins. The adrenaline was blocking all my thoughts. The shock took me beyond thought. All I had was prayer. And then, just like that, it was over. I opened my eyes and saw my colt standing and shivering before me.

I led Far Go to the corral and saw that he had only skinned his hide. There was to be no dying horse or broken bones in the canyon that day. I turned him loose and dropped to my knees. I wept like I had never wept before. So many thoughts ran through my mind. Of course I felt great relief that Far Go wasn't hurt and that he was out of the trailer. But this experience also reminded me of the great responsibility I held for these horses. Ray used to say, "I can't teach experience," and I really began to wonder if I had enough experience to keep us all safe. I was alone and living in a canyon. Should I be taking on these unknown and unforeseen troubles? The what-ifs plagued my thoughts. I then spoke with the One who showed Himself to me in my moment of need. I asked God if I was cut out for this life. I sincerely considered quitting. For the first time ever, since achieving my lifelong dream of living with horses, I was willing to give it up. I considered letting it all go.

This willingness to let it all go was my surrender. I was surrendering to the truth that life is not predictable. It wasn't going to be simple or easy, and it might even be frightening and painful. I was surrendering to the truth of my own vulnerability. I had to be willing to accept what is and accept myself right where I was. Surrendering to what is, is a spiritual awakening. Not all surrender is necessarily voluntary. Sometimes the circumstances of life offer enough friction that they force us to make heartfelt decisions. Are we all in, or are we dealing ourselves out? There is something very liberating about coming to a crossroads in life and making a commitment.

A Fresh Start

Soon after I surrendered to my thoughts of whether I was tough enough, there came a new sense of freedom. This sense of freedom somehow penetrated and healed the wounds of my painful experience. No longer did I work with my horses from simply an intellectual standpoint. The bond had been made. I chose them. I had dropped to my knees and from there learned to stand. I chose my relationship with the horse, with God as my witness. I committed to my passion in the ceremony of rebirth from a painful past.

At this point in my journey, I had been attending Ray Hunt clinics for many years—though I had never ridden in one. I had always made excuses not to ride. Humans have a knack for validating fears. We can always find reasons to stay stuck where we are. For me, the best change comes from desire. Desire upstages the comfortable mediocrity of the mind. The mind wants things to be predictable, safe, and secure. Desire encourages dancing where habits fear to tread. "Change is good" is the heart's motto, while the fear-based conventional mind whispers, "Wouldn't it be easier to pass?" Thoughts of limited time and money are typically the supporting details in our excuses to stay safe. Each time Ray Hunt came to offer his brilliant guidance, I would say, "I just can't afford it." That was until I awoke from my surrender. This was a new day, and I chose a new way.

Two months after Far Go had flipped himself in the trailer, I found myself hauling him for three hours to finally ride with the master teacher Ray Hunt. I borrowed a big, open stock trailer and hauled him untied. I hoped that God was still on call. We arrived in Eugene, Oregon, after dark and found the barn. It was a huge facility with dozens of temporary stalls to house the many horses that had been brought to meet the master. This was a world into which neither Far Go nor I had ever ventured. The next morning would come all too soon. I sensed that we were both in for a sleepless night.

Surrendering to what is, is a spiritual awakening.

Nerves do not suffice to describe the feeling I had in my bones, the rattling of the senses and the lump lodged squarely in my throat. It was as if I were riding for the pope. Yet I had no idea why. I found myself there with simply the intentions to survive. My highest level of ambition was that at the end of the clinic Ray Hunt would say, "Mary who?" I just wanted both Far Go and me to be invisible. A good ride was a noneventful ride. Ray Hunt was known for being direct, to say the least. I had asked him questions when I audited clinics in the past, so at least I had that experience in opening myself up to Ray. The first thing I recall at this clinic was that two big draft horses had arrived in a trailer and the person couldn't get them out. So Ray and all his devotees wandered out to the parking lot, and he proceeded to unload them. After Ray unloaded those two horses, I thought this was the opportunity to tell him about what I had experienced with Far Go flipping over. It was frankly hard to believe. There I was, just two months later, standing next to Ray Hunt with Far Go saddled and ready to ride.

I shared with Ray that I didn't know what had gone wrong. I explained that Far Go had previously been hauled several times and that he had loaded just fine the day that he flipped over. I shared that I felt so lost and full of guilt and that I felt it was my lack of experience that was to blame. Ray listened, with that Ray Hunt twinkle in his eye. I expected to hear a list of things I could have done or perhaps a list of should-nots. Instead Ray Hunt offered kind compassion with his reply. I'll not forget the words he used when he said, "Well...sometimes you just need to go in, have your breakfast, and take a fresh start." And then he said with a wink, "But you got him here, didn't you?"

Far Go and I had a fantastic time at the clinic. I felt that he stayed with me mentally each step of the way. On the last day, as Ray was giving his final talk, I decided to step down and stand beside Far Go. It had been quite a week. Just as I was swinging my leg over him to step off, someone sitting on the viewing deck above us crumpled up a potato chip bag. This crackling, unfamiliar sound from above his head sent Far Go sailing several feet from the stands. I was in mid-swing when he spooked. Fortunately, I simply regained my seat and settled my horse. Although I knew Ray saw the whole thing, he never missed a word of what he was saying. I was grateful that we didn't end our positive experience by me falling off my horse, especially during Ray's closing comments. I was glad for me, of course, but I was really glad for Far Go. We stayed together through it all. I rode a few steps and then stepped down. It was a good place to quit. It was time for me and my horse to go home and unpack all that we had learned.

The next day I made my breakfast and remembered that my teacher had taught me to take a fresh start. He didn't say avoid pain or don't take chances. I took what Ray said to mean "live life." We are presented each day with choices. Sometimes these choices look like roadblocks. Sometimes those roadblocks require our willingness to understand life (or our experiences) at a deeper level. I learned the true value of what I loved by experiencing my surrender from holding tightly to it. When we rally with willingness and authentically surrender to a traumatic life experience, we grow. In this authentic way, we don't simply go through pain; we grow through it.

Life isn't easy. It's not meant to make us happy; it is meant to make us grow up. I grew into my own courage. It was there when I reached for it. And when the student is ready, the master appears. There he was in battered chaps and a dusty hat, holding a toothpick in his teeth. Ray's infectious grin still guides me when life begins pulling me to my knees. The answers are just as real now as they were when I was standing in that parking lot, surrounded by fear and guided by my willingness to learn. I still have my witness—I know I can ask God for help.

Releasing the past is at the heart of perfect practice. Clinging to our past can keep us bound to outdated, ineffective habits and fearful perceptions. I had a lot of past to forgive and forget. I grew through this experience with Far Go because of the pain I had experienced, not in spite of it. I understood the value of what I was doing with my life. I was deeply grateful for the guidance of my teacher, and I had the experience of transcending what I perceived as failure. This experience offered me something that would help me forevermore, not just with Far Go but also in life. I learned I didn't have to settle for fear.

When we live from old perceptions, it's easy to repeat the same mistakes over and over without realizing why we keep having the same outcomes. Much of the time we are unconscious of how we actually re-create these situations. At each Ray Hunt clinic that I attended, I heard Ray remind folks that it is the human who has to change. People tend to think it's the horse (or life) that must change in order to have peace. Now I truly realize the power and the genius in Ray's statement.

All too often, we judge the horse for being wrong or bad or undisciplined without taking ownership for our part. This happens in life as well. We view our circumstances as undesirable, yet we don't create a change. The path to peace is to know our response-ability. When faced with a difficult situation, we have three choices. We can accept it, change it, or leave it. The fundamentally transformative element in this process is that we choose consciously.

The Creative Process

We direct and build our life through our own creative process. To have the life we want, we first have to be aware that our experiences are created through our perceptions. It is how we relate to life (or the horse) that creates our experience. Life gets really exciting when we realize we can use our own dynamic energy to create exactly what we want. We can utilize pain as our teacher. Pain teaches us through contrast. When a horse (or life) bucks us off and leaves us in the dirt, we have a clear picture of what we don't want. This experience is opposite of what we do want. The clear contrast can help us understand the importance of doing things differently. Limitations arise when we only focus on our experience through fearing it. Releasing the past means learning from it and then letting it go.

We all want to feel a sense of joy, peace, and unity. Our feelings are our indicators. Feelings of harmony mirror back to us that we are on the right track! Horses are indicators to us as well. It can be really obvious when riding a horse if we are effective or ineffective. When we experience those rides where a thousand pounds of athletic force don't weigh anything in our hands, when there is no resistance, the feeling is wonderful. These are the rides in life that confirm for us what we really want. Tom would say, "If I could get them to feel it, they would reach for it again and again." When I feel unity with my horses, it certainly inspires me to reach for that feel again and again. In life and in horses, perfect practice is about being very present in the moments that feel united. It is building on the good feelings and then, through practice, stringing them together; we call this counting the good strides.

To have the life we want, we first have to be aware that our experiences are created through our perceptions.

We have the freedom to choose where to apply our attention. Resistance and fear are experienced when we relate the present to a painful past. There is a biological tendency to stay focused on pain. We are naturally wired to focus on danger or resistance. If we touch fire, we get burned, so we learn not to touch it again. In this way fear can be beneficial. As an unconscious habit, though, it loses its effectiveness and becomes dysfunctional. Living from unconscious fear builds our lives from a negative perspective. Fear is very energetic and stimulating, and it can get a lot of our attention.

Life can be exceptionally gratifying when we realize that our thoughts create our interactions and our interactions create our relationships—and that to truly relate is what living is all about. There is a long bridge that spans the process of creating what we want. The past is at one end of the bridge, and the future is at the other. In between are gradient degrees from denial to understanding, and this is where it's beneficial to focus our awareness. Do we recognize what our part was in the outcome we didn't want? If we don't see our contribution to each situation, we can (and most likely will) repeat it in the future. We will move to the next horse or job or relationship with the same habits that create what we don't want.

Releasing the past in perfect practice means fully understanding (through hindsight) what led us into the experience in the first place. What were our reactions to the situation, and what did we do to survive? What were the unconscious habits that came to the surface? We can notice our emotions and responses and see how they affect all our relationships. The awareness of our part allows us to bring conscious intent to our life. With this practice, we utilize pain to create wisdom. Ray joked about never making the same mistake twice and laughed that he was too busy making new ones. He must have known there was value in learning from his mistakes. Perfect practice is mindfully making the changes that our mistakes show us that we need to make.

An interesting tendency that becomes evident in the relationship with horse and human is, when something isn't working, people might resort to doing more of it. If a person feels they can't control a horse, they often get a more severe bit, a bigger spur, a chain, or a whip. This creates even more pressure and pain for the horse. This unconscious tendency toward force is very sad and shows what the unaware mind does in a forceful state. It is no different in life. In conversations where we feel we are not being heard, we can resort to yelling, insisting, debating, or just walking away. This tendency actually separates us from what we want. We can end up feeling even more alone, unvalued, or unheard. Rather than increasing our resistance, we can pause and seek to understand the influence we are having on the situation. Sometimes pausing or doing less in itself can create a positive change.

Awakening to the Habit of Defense

Resistance is a limiting reaction that closes the mind and restricts our options. Unknowingly we can easily continue to practice the habit of defense. My unconscious tendency came from my distant past. When I felt alone and separated, I put my hands up in defense and added more resistance. This only confirmed my fear and feelings of separation. It certainly did not teach me to connect. I started this habit as a young child and continued it into my adult life.

I was five years old when my parents divorced. Shortly after, my father remarried and moved to Jamaica. I couldn't understand this dramatic change in my life, and no one explained it to me. I could only assume it was my fault. At that age the world was very small, and I thought everything was about me. I longed for my father to return and dreamed of mailing myself to him in a great big box.

Not long after he left the country, my father and his new wife had a daughter. I hadn't seen him for a couple of years. Then one day a letter came in the mail. Letters from my father were like gold, as they were few and far between. In the letter was a photograph. There he was kneeling on the beach looking so happy and holding his toddler daughter in his arms. Even as a young girl, my fears seemed to take over my reality. All I could imagine when I saw the picture was that he had traded me in for a better daughter. This photo was the proof to my young mind that I was indeed unwanted by the man who mattered most. Not long after receiving this letter, I started acting out in school and even bullied other children. I became exactly what I feared to be true. I became that bad child.

Fear closes doors. Those doors keep us separated, and separation is what created the resistance in the first place. Fear and reactivity are a perfect example of a vicious cycle. I couldn't have known about this as a child. But as an adult I began to see this cycle in my life. It was an enlightening day when I finally became aware of my tendency to unconsciously add to my problems. Just the recognition of this habit felt like freedom. That's when I started to see that what I was creating was exactly what I didn't want. It would be comical if it weren't so painful. My awareness of the cycle opened my heart and offered with it a brand-new way of living.

Ray would often ask us if we could do less and get more done. Instead of using more force to achieve an outcome, I learned to pause and allow it a little more time. Sometimes in becoming rigid and focusing on an agenda, it is easy to lose our feel for a situation. When I pause I can open my mind and find alternative options.

Eventually my half sister and I became very close. Although we have different mothers, there are many similarities between us. These traits brought me closer to knowing my father. I could see in her what I, too, inherited from him. As an adult I went to visit my sister in her home in California. There I had a chance to unlearn my past and face that ancient fear. On a bedside table in a frame was the same photo that I had received as a child. I burst into tears. Thirty years later I allowed the tears that (for lack of understanding) I never cried as a child. The child in me simply assimilated the pain. That day in California I let go of believing that it was me who had caused my father to leave our family and go off to start a new one.

When I focus on outcomes rather than the process, I lose sight of the present moment and all its value. My reactions to a troubling situation feel very real and give me an illusion of knowing. It's easy to believe that we don't have a choice. But it is the reactivity that is keeping us stuck and closing our minds, not the world in which we live. The reactivity is forcing us to focus on what we don't want.

Behind the veil of my reaction was a truer vision. I didn't lose my heart in that painful situation, though at times it felt like I had. My reactivity to the pain was simply in the way. Once I understood this pattern in my life, it was easier to see from a deeper perspective. The world seemed to be a safer place when I didn't assume the worst from it. And it wasn't long after this realization that I began creating what I loved rather than fostering what I feared.

When I focus on outcomes rather than the process, I lose sight of the present moment and all its value.

Endless Potential

When I watched Ray Hunt ride a horse, I could barely see his cues. I didn't believe I could ever ride like that. So I didn't. I took from the experience what fit for me at the time. Looking back, I realize that was barely a fraction of what Ray offered. Now, all these years later, that picture in my mind still plays. In the quiet and solitude of my arena, I have begun to do so much less. Now I believe in my horse, and together we explore endless options. When we let go of our rigid opinions about our limitations, we can be open to the potential within us. Being open allows us to reach beyond our limitations and set the bar a bit higher with each success.

Ray Hunt said, "The horse is truth."

Truth is. Life is. The horse doesn't lie. He will mirror back to us our abilities and disabilities. And in this mirror is the greatest teaching of profound wisdom we can imagine—if we will allow it. Life teaches us how to live, yet we often run from it, mask it, cloak it, resist it, and deny it. All the while life keeps offering us opportunities for a new perspective. Acceptance and open-mindedness offer us not only better options but also the wisdom that comes from experience.

Problems tend to arise when there is no guidance for our emotions. Without a positive direction, we can get really lost in feelings of fear, insecurity, sadness, and helplessness. Pretty soon it seems that we don't have feelings but rather feelings have us. The biological response of fight, flight, or freeze takes over our lives just to keep the ship from sinking. This is why people might feel the need to escape—sometimes through using drugs or alcohol. When we sense there are limited options to feeling good, escape seems pretty reasonable. The lack of better options is also why sometimes horses buck; they don't have a better deal before them. I know both Ray and Tom pointed this out when they mentioned (in general) that bucking is the last thing the horse wants to do! This can be difficult for people to understand, especially if it's the first thing the horse does. Perhaps by realizing we have the same defensive tendency in our own life, we can better empathize with the horse. We can seek first to understand ourselves and horses better and let compassion guide our choices.

No one is wrong for not knowing what the better options are. Where would we have learned to deal with our feelings? We learned math, science, and history. But I don't remember a stress management class in school. I do remember detention hall, and I visited it many times. You see, I was that bucking horse. I completely understand and relate to feeling lost, though that hardship in life has led me to the greatest sense of love and peace I can imagine. The contrast teaches—if we'll let it.

I learned to be tough in my childhood, and I held true to this as I went out on my own. I learned to cope by holding on to all the control. My motto was "If it's to be, it's up to me." This felt like a good, strong trait for an independent woman. But what I came to realize was that it was also what kept me from asking for help. I wouldn't let anyone in. Fear had built a strong barricade, and I was not yielding. One evening when I was feeding my horses, I learned just how frightening not accepting help from others could be. I had been experiencing some back pain, and I was in a habit of just pushing through it. I had a lot of work to do and no patience for being weak. As I walked with the grain buckets down the steep, muddy hill to the barn, I felt the familiar burning pain in the small of my back. I had already entered the shed when I heard the horses running toward it. Right about then the muscles spasmed, and the searing pain sent me right to my knees. The buckets and grain went sailing, and the herd was on the run. I could not get to my feet before they all came running into the shed. I could only hope they would not run me over.

As I crawled to the wall and pulled myself up, I had a reality check. I could see my habit of independence had its dark side. The next morning a friend came and drove me to the chiropractor. I talked about how I realized that this tendency came from the little girl who felt unworthy of her father's love. I was still punishing myself for that. It was time to make a change. And this humbling walk up the ramp to the chiropractor was just the first of many steps.

Releasing my past offers me freedom to expand my awareness and cultivate a learning frame of mind. Releasing the past is forgiveness. In release I forgive my shortcomings and those of others. Unencumbered by the limited perceptions of my past, I was free to open my mind. That increased my opportunities for new experiences. These new experiences enriched my life and gave me the chance to expand my knowledge and see a greater purpose.

Taking a fresh start, I launched my future from a place of freedom. I set the bar just a little higher and didn't settle for less. I broadened my perspective. With the forgiveness of a fresh start, I even found myself standing before the master teacher, in the perfect setting, primed to learn. And I've been learning ever since.

With understanding came forgiveness, and with forgiveness came my freedom.

With understanding came forgiveness, and with forgiveness came my freedom. I feel confident this is a firm foundation for a well-lived life. And then who knows, one day when we least expect it, we may witness the unimaginable. We may allow our potential the wings it needs to realize the dream we hold within. The horse has held his potential within him all along. He is just waiting for us to catch up.

Chapter Four

The Shift from Obligation to Dedication

A S A CHILD I WAS CALLED A LATCHKEY KID. MY MOTHER raised four children alone, and she worked long hours to do it. My siblings were considerably older, and I would often come home to an empty house. I seemed to be a magnet for stray animals. Dogs, cats, mice—you name it, I brought it home. An empty house in the suburbs was not a favorable environment for keeping pets. Each time a dog followed me home, I pled my case to my mother with great enthusiasm. Each time my pleas were met with the same verdict, given with love and an undeniable list of substantiating evidence. My overburdened mother would say, "I'm sorry, Mary, the answer is still no." Looking back, I think this is where I began to form my strong desire for the word *yes*. Seldom do I settle for *no* as an answer in my life. I feel this is one reason I have been so successful in building the life I want.

I watched as the animals streamed through my young life like sand in a windstorm. I never gave up my desire to connect with them. I struggled with letting go of what I loved. The conflict in this prompted a lot of pain. I felt more and more detached. Through it all my heart held true to its passion. I was driven to overcome the sense of separation.

In my childhood I was no stranger to lonesomeness. The one place that I truly felt I belonged was with these defenseless stray animals. I felt a sense of purpose caring for strays. They were as lonesome as I was. Some of my best friends were a hairless cat, a dog that resembled a hyena with paws bloody from hot asphalt, and a mouse found covered with ants. I related to all the misfits. We became kindred spirits. In these friends, I found myself.

The kinship I felt with these animals came from deep within my heart. It was not so much of a logical or thought-out commitment; it was more like breathing. It came through me naturally. Unfortunately the dichotomy was that these relationships were fleeting and always ended in wailing tears of separation. My mother was kind, loving, and nurturing. I am sure that seeing her child on the roller coaster of love and loss devoured her heart as well. She was also a smart, resourceful, and effective parent and found an organization that would find good homes for all the strays. The organization Friends of Animals became a bridge for us through this emotional journey. At a very early age, I began to learn the hard lesson of letting go. I feverishly fed the dream that one day I wouldn't have to say goodbye. This early experience is what set up my life's dedication.

I often told my mother that I longed for horses. She replied lovingly, "There, there, Mary. All little girls dream of ponies." I knew in my heart this was different. This was not a whim but a calling. As a child, I never convinced her. I was twenty-two when I bought my first horse and moved to the country. This act of following my heart set precedent for my future and guided me on my essential inward journey.

Today, living with horses offers a lifestyle I cherish. It is a life bursting with beautiful moments. Living close to nature, I experience romantic rides through mountain streams leading into stands of cedars smelling of incense in the sun. I have spent countless summer evenings simply listening to the meditative sounds of horses munching peacefully on their hay. And still the child in me revels at the sense of belonging I feel on frosty winter mornings coming into the barn to the sound of welcoming nickers.

Along with this lifestyle also comes a great deal of hard work. Simply put: manual labor. There is a responsibility to the herd. There are fences to fix, stalls to muck, and hay to buck. There are injuries, illnesses, and even an occasional mournful loss. There are early mornings and long days. All in all, it is an obligation of time, money, heart, and soul. The intense significance of my lifestyle, combined with the contrast of joy and hardship, has offered me a provocative look into the mechanics of a dedicated life.

The Alchemy of Dedication

Each day (little by little) I grow, learn, evolve, shift, and morph into a new understanding and a greater awareness. The more I enjoy life, the more excited I am learning about it. The more I learn, the easier things become. Much like horsemanship, life is an education. I had no problem dedicating myself to horses. They are what inspire me. I didn't always have that same feeling of dedication for day-to-day living. Going to work, paying the bills, and keeping a household could easily feel mundane or tedious. That was until I learned the powerful difference between dedication and obligation.

I never saw feeding the horses and the dogs or cleaning the barn as chores. In fact, it was just the opposite. I felt like I was making a cozy life for us all. I loved providing for the animals. I started to see the difference in how it felt caring for them as opposed to caring for myself. I would easily call the vet out if a horse was sick, but I would rarely go to the doctor. I would make sure the horses' feet were trimmed and their dental work done, but I wouldn't go to the dentist or buy a new pair of boots. It was easy to see the contrast in all of this. I identified it as the difference between dedication and obligation. I was not dedicated to caring for myself. The obligation of my life felt heavy, but I was dedicated to making other lives happy. This had to change for me to enjoy all aspects of living. And it did as I began to recognize the benefits of dedication.

For those of us who love horses, working with them is no work at all. I heard a friend of Ray's (and a great teacher in his own right) once say, "It's what a fella would do for a living if he didn't have to make a living." I then began to understand the power that dedication has in our lives. It can transform the dirt to gold. It changes our "should" to "want," and this is alchemy of the richest form.

I don't hold resistance about the time and money I spend on the farm because I am living from my heart. I am dedicated to the animals and to our home—and I enjoy what I do. Without my dedication, building fences, cleaning stalls, and spending the money it takes to run the farm would most certainly seem like burdens.

I understand that my intention (or inspiration) holds the power to transform my world. With this awareness, I orchestrate my life. This is an essential lesson in realizing my perfect practice. Once I understood that I could choose to see my own role in life as either a burden or a gift, I unleashed a great power within me. I went from feeling like a victim to being excited. I began to look at everything I did, checking in to see if I was acting from obligation or dedication. I ran all my life's components through this filter.

Practicing dedication allowed me to see how many things I did out of habit. I also noticed I had adopted other people's opinions, perceptions, and standards for my life. For example, I found I really didn't like eating meat. I ate it because that was what I had been taught. I began to shed many outdated habits just by recognizing how I really felt. Living authentically brought inspiration to all areas of my life. I consider this time of recognition to be a new birth of sorts—a brand-new incarnation.

Ray Hunt taught Alchemy of Dedication through the undeniable changes in the horse's reactions and behaviors. It is hard to imagine a more archaic practice than domination over another living creature. Ray always reminded us that we are working with a mind. He showed us that our horses are alive—they are breathing and thinking and reacting just like we are. They have bodies that get sick and well. Since I live with horses every day, I also see that it is true that they do indeed have good days and bad days. They get tired and irritated, inspired and motivated. People somehow forget this and try to force them to do things without considering how horses really feel. This can cause a lot of grief, not only for the horse but for the person as well.

At his clinics Ray would get us to see it from the horse's perspective, and then everything would begin to change. He showed us how tapping into the horse's own desire for well-being offered us success we never thought imaginable. When we shifted our approach from "You should do this" to "It's in your best interest," the horse began to see the value, and his ambition increased. Ray would encourage us to show the horse how easy life was when we operated in partnership. This meant we had to honor our part in it.

The development of trust is a sacred experience, and it comes from dedication of the heart, whereas obligation comes from thoughts and paradigms of the mind. The heart holds compassion, empathy, and acceptance. These qualities are all attributes of dedication and come from unconditioned love. This dynamism comes from feeling, not from an agenda. Dedication inspires creativity. When we approach life from this perspective, we can find miracles in everyday activities. I realized a fulfilled

life isn't really about the things I do—it is about how I *feel* when
I am doing the things I do.

Building Trust

Early in my experience with horses, there came a turning point
in understanding how empathy, compassion, and acceptance
can build a dedicated relationship. In this early experience I
found my friend, teacher, and partner for this journey—my
horse Cayenne. Together we took the rough clay of our desire
for well-being and formed it into a vessel of emerging unity.

When I first met Cayenne, it was midsummer, and her barn
was a good hour's drive from my home. During these trips I
drove an old '65 Chevy pickup that lacked air-conditioning and
was a bit short on comfort. I felt dedicated to visiting her at
least every other day, as she was alone in a dusty arena. She
was dragging a ten-foot rope. The people selling her said they
couldn't catch her, and frankly I noticed they were afraid of her.
She was just a baby, only six months old. This period in my life
was deeply emotional. I wanted to have children, though I was
in a tumultuous marriage, and we were not successful conceiv-
ing. I felt frightened, alone, and unsure about where my life
was heading. I felt lost. The moment I saw this little colt and
recognized her resistance to those around her, I related to that
feeling and responded with a deep, heartfelt empathy.

I felt surprised by the lack of awareness in the man selling
this young colt. He was breeding horses to sell, yet he seemed to
know very little about their nature. He claimed he and another
man had tried to trim her feet. They were hopelessly unsuccess-
ful. There was blood on the wall of her stall, and I wondered
whose it was—hers or theirs? She had just been weaned from
her mother and separated from all the horses. I can't imagine the

sense of insecurity she must have had to overcome. In six short months, alone in her stall, Cayenne had learned the strongest source of resistance on the planet: separation.

The development of trust is a sacred experience, and it comes from dedication of the heart, whereas obligation comes from thoughts and paradigms of the mind.

The main person in Cayenne's life, the man who owned the breeding farm, was also the same one promoting her sense of separation. He would open the door to the stall and drive her down the alleyway. Cayenne was dragging the long rope in case she had to be captured. She spent her days in the arena and her nights in a stall. There was no grazing or horseplay. She was just alone and fearful of the only source of her survival. I am sure she felt great conflict. The ability to adapt to life and to hardship is a lesson we can all learn well from horses. Horses (even babies) accept and forgive as their everyday practice. In contrast, the human ego expects and blames as its practice. This ego tendency perpetuates an obligatory mind that can easily separate us from our true dedication.

There is no doubt in my mind that our horses mirror our deepest feelings. Ray openly conveyed that he could tell a lot about a person by looking at their horse. I have to say that I sense that correlation as well. I also see that same kind of connection within our lives. Our jobs, relationships, homes, and lifestyles all speak volumes as to our beliefs about ourselves on an internal level. The conditions of our life will tell us what our deepest feelings have to say. Of course we habitually acclimate ourselves to believe our feelings come from our conditions—not that our conditions come from our feelings.

I knew it was no coincidence that I wanted to rescue this child horse. I had always covertly wanted to be rescued although I came out fighting, just like Cayenne. I had built a strong defense early in life. Now I am spending the rest of my life learning a different way. Horses seem to learn much quicker.

I did not want to start my relationship with Cayenne by throwing her into a trailer and adding more to her traumatic beginning. I offered to buy her with the condition that I teach her to lead before taking her home. Day after day I worked with her in the big open arena. It was late August, hot and dusty, and she was determined to resist. Never having owned a colt and being very young in my education with horses, I was anxious to nurture this youngster. I had saved up so much maternal instinct that I thought I might just die from it. I wished she could see that I was there to help, but I also realized how hard it was for her to trust. I felt such empathy for her. And even though I was close enough to grab the ten-foot rope, I didn't. This was the beginning of a lifelong relationship, and I wanted it to be her choice as well as mine.

Finally, after many visits, she approached me with great trepidation. As I gently walked up to her, I simply unsnapped the rope she had been dragging, turned around, and walked away. I hung the rope on the fence on my way out and went home. I will never forget her expression in that moment. She was sure I was going to grab her when I got close enough, yet she stayed and braced herself for it. The longing for trust was so strong that it overshadowed her fear. This can be true for all of us. It may be that we just don't feel safe enough to open ourselves to those who extend a hand in kindness. Or perhaps we don't recognize them. We don't believe we can be safe, secure, or trusting. This moment was the beginning of my journey to the center of my heart. And Cayenne became my guru.

The next time I came out to see my new colt, she stepped forward to meet me. From then on we allowed that trust to grow. That is not to say we didn't experience fear, rejection, reaction, defense, and a multitude of other emotions. We had countless experiences that could easily have caused separation and fear. But we had the foundation we had both built on trust. As long as I kept the intention on respect and my values on the acceptance of allowing us to be right where we were, we grew. Cayenne became a trustworthy teacher with little children and novice riders. When I would bring a small child in to meet her and handed the child the lead rope, Cayenne would lower her head to be just as tall as the child. She passed on the lessons of overcoming fear to those who came into her life. This, too, is my mirror and the basis for this book. We teach what we most desire to learn.

The Paradigm of Incompleteness

Embryotic life gives us an early education in the essence of dedication. From the moment of conception, we have within us the perfect heart of acceptance. We have no expectations of growth—we just grow! We float along, dedicated to living. Living in dedication is a very natural process. The problem arises soon after birth, when we begin to lose track of this natural talent. We actually learn to ignore the pure essence of life itself. We forget that life has a natural course. We lose sight of our own inner navigator and begin to rely on beliefs and perceptions. In the womb, we didn't have to "make something happen"—we allowed it.

We are born into a physical world with a focus on dependency. Like any other living thing, we begin our quest for survival. We immediately acquire perceptions of scarcity and striving. This is greatly attributed to biological survival responses. At a very young age, beliefs of "not enough" and "I'll be happy when" influence our outlook. Hunger triggers a need for nourishment, cold a need for warmth. The human intellect (and its survival responses) senses the feeling of incompleteness. Intellectually this all leads to a life zeroed in on the insufficient moment. These perceptions are not right or wrong, or good or bad; they are simply incomplete. We know something is amiss. And since the idea of scarcity is biologically imprinted, we prematurely assume this sense of incompleteness is our identity. We then find validating proof that we are lacking as individuals, and we maintain that, indeed, there is not enough. From this perspective, we don't realize that we have simply forgotten our true heart's content—the place of acceptance that is our guiding life force.

This deeply ingrained paradigm is one way we obscure our natural connection to dedication and fulfillment. Knowing that life is complete in each moment is the antidote to my thoughts of scarcity. Things aren't always black and white. There are many shades in between. Ray and Tom were brilliant in recognizing the slightest change. They knew that from moment to moment things changed and within that changing environment was an opportunity to learn and improve. What they knew about horses applied to life as well. I found that when I paid close attention to each breath, I could have a fresh new start from moment to moment. I realized there were a thousand lifetimes in a day.

We each still have within us the effective, peaceful, and fulfilling essence of where we came from. If we try, we can return to that early model of seeing our world as inter-reliant. We can feel the perfect unity in all things. This may take some practice, since we have lived from this incompleteness for a long time. But practice is what this book is all about.

I was tied down by the habit of obligation. Feeling obligated is a heavy burden. Obligation takes away the vast array of choices that each moment offers. The feeling that I was incomplete limited my mobility. My old ways of thinking would sometimes creep back in when I wasn't looking. It was as if I would forget what it was that made life feel so much better. Old habits left a trail behind me that my mind would try to follow. Living from my outdated, incomplete thoughts was like driving a car by looking in the rearview mirror. It is only effective in reverse.

Living from my outdated, incomplete thoughts was like driving a car by looking in the rearview mirror. It is only effective in reverse.

One of my all-time favorite Ray Hunt quotes is "The horse learns what he lives, and he lives it the way he learns it." This brilliantly described to me how easy it is to unconsciously learn and develop habits. We learn what we practice. To feel a sense of dedication, I had to "practice" dedication. At the very least, I had to be aware of the difference between defense and acceptance, or obligation and dedication. As soon as I became aware of my practice, I quickly saw my patterns. I saw that what I do, how I think, and what I feel don't always align. I realized obligation comes from the habit of intellectual sacrifice. Dedication comes from the practice of willingly giving and receiving from the heart. This is a fine line, though a vastly cavernous one. I can learn to overcome thoughts of fear, scarcity, and defense—and remember feeling complete. A dedicated life is one that stems from feeling fulfilled. It is not conditional on being enough.

Ray Hunt was in no popularity contest. He made it clear that first and foremost he was there for the horse. Ray's genius was in his unending dedication. He didn't try to become something he wasn't. He built right from where he was. He knew he had something important and valuable. He didn't need another's validation to know this. Many people had opinions about how he "should" be doing things. He was in no way obligated to anyone. Sometimes this put people off. I saw this transparency as refreshing. I never fit in well with the popular consensus, and I admired his willingness to be authentic.

Nature is a place where we can easily learn to release the tendency to fix things. Standing by an ocean, we rarely see it as incomplete. To the contrary, the experience often leads to a sense of fulfillment. Standing before a beautiful sunset, I feel a heightened sense of excitement. Acceptance peaks when I am in awe of natural beauty. I celebrate the moment. I don't say, "I wish it had a tad more orange," or "It's a little on the small side, don't you think?" The feeling of reverential acceptance is always accessible. It does not come from something or someone outside of us. We were born from pure inspiration, and our last breath will return us there. My task is to fill in the middle with my own innate ability to see from the heart of dedication.

CHAPTER FIVE

Willingness

A NUTRITIONIST ONCE TOLD ME THAT THE BEST FRUITS and vegetables to eat are the ones with blemishes. He said there is actually a positive cellular effect that comes from the survival response or healing practice of the fruit, a "beating the odds," so to speak. In these "less than perfect" specimens is a willingness to heal and to grow. I love the wisdom in this perception and immediately saw it as an analogy for many things, health and well-being taking center stage.

I know I am not alone when I say I have considered myself somewhat of a bruised fruit. It has been a lifelong adventure to reinvent myself in a light with which I honor, respect, and appreciate who I am, blemishes and all. This is still a work in progress, though now I can see where my ancient bruises have taught me survival. I learned so much more than resilience and strength. Being battered by life events offered me opportunities to find a state of surrender that opened my ultimate will not just for having well-being but also for learning it.

Just the other day I witnessed a great example of recognizing well-being through the contrast of distress. My young horse Poco is at the bottom of the herd's pecking order. On that day I noticed every horse had been picking on him. Eventually he was even shunned from the feed area and was standing in the corner of the pasture. Poco is definitely the "little brother," and sometimes he pushes his luck. I didn't see everything that happened before what I saw happen, but he was definitely singled out. I went out to get him for a ride, and when I haltered him, he was jumpy and flinchy. I could see the fear in his eyes. I knew I had better pay close attention to how he was feeling during our ride. He seemed to be in a vulnerable state.

Poco and I walked into the arena, and I noticed he was instantly relaxing. He lowered his high head, and he started letting out deep breaths, sighing and blowing. This was a strong contrast to what I had seen just a moment earlier. It was also not at all what I had expected. I really paused to ponder what this change was all about. I quickly realized that it was a state of grace, if you will, a sense of security that came through him. He felt at peace with me.

Poco had come to me as a bit of a bruised fruit; he had seen starvation and violence in his young life. I have made it a point to always give him a safe place to be. The arena is our playground and a sanctuary from the difficulties of life. It is where we con-nect—emotionally, spiritualty, and physically. When we entered the arena, he could feel at ease and safe. He could leave his wor-ries behind. I often hear this from people who visit me in the canyon. As they start down the long, winding road that curves and twists through the trees, nestled and tucked into the earth's rolling soil, they feel they can leave their worries at the gate. Life seems to take on a brand-new feel. The secret, I tell them, is to carry that feel back into the world when they leave. This speaks very strongly to the difference between having peace and finding it. It is the difference between dependency and will. Dependency is always on something outside of us. Will is opening to the peace that resides within.

To observe contrast is to see differences. Polarities such as good and bad or dark and light offer us the ability to label and compare. Comparison is how we evaluate what we want from what we don't want. When I know this, I can see conflict as a positive thing. I can see it as a strong indicator pointing to what I want. If something is ineffective, I can ponder what would be effective through contrast. Life became much more pleasurable when I could see hardship as a tool and anger as a pathway to peace.

Dependency is always on something outside of us. Will is opening to the peace that resides within.

Poco's conflict was an example of what I feel is the ultimate contrast in life: fear and love. It was plain to see that Poco was really starting to hunt up feeling good. He now knows there is a flip side to fear. Good is also a choice. It is natural and common to focus on fear. Fear is where many of us lose sight of our well-being. We are geared to protect ourselves, yet we become victims of life if we don't see there are always at least two choices in contrast and in conflict.

I have mentioned how we can hold on to historic opinions about our fears. Opinions and perceptions come through a myriad of input. A great deal of this input is the perception of our environment. Dependency on our environment is not a perception of will but a reliance on circumstance. This dependency can feel like the opposite of freedom. I know that when I am dependent on something or someone, that dependency seems to carry with it a residing fear of loss. What happens if...? However, my will holds limitless freedom within it. I used to believe I had to search outside myself for this feeling of completeness. I have definitely looked for love in all the wrong places. But through that contrast I finally realized I had lost myself in the search. I once heard a story of a beggar sitting on a box asking for handouts. After he died the townspeople unlocked the box and found it was full of gold nuggets. He had never looked inside. He never knew his wealth. This symbolizes what can happen when we focus our well-being outside of us.

Reclaiming free will takes practice. This is one reason perfect practice is so vitally important. If we practice defense and protection rather than seeing an alternate route, we end up wearing fear like our skin. We can learn to accept things. When Ray Hunt started colts, he helped them learn to accept the things that could be frightening, such as wearing a saddle. He wanted them to feel as good about the saddle as they did about their mane and tail. At first, the saddle can seem very threatening to horses. They can build a great practice of gaining confidence by being shown they have a choice. We say, "You get in and you get out." In other words, releasing the pressure and allowing them to learn to accept is vital to success. We may just use the saddle pad to get them accustomed to the saddle. Lay the pad on their back, and then we can go to the saddle. Maybe just put the saddle on and off without cinching it down. And then move ahead incrementally. This is very important to the horse. By breaking down the steps—practicing—it is a lot easier to assimilate and to understand.

That morning, Poco demonstrated to me that he knew there was another way that he could feel. He didn't have to do what he always did. He could trust, and in trusting he could enjoy a learning frame of mind. This is why I find horses to be such a great metaphor for life. We can gain so much from looking into the eyes of contrast. When we look at contrast in a horse, it can be pretty undeniable.

Ray spoke of horses turning loose. To me, turning loose is the effect of willingness and an open mind. Turning loose originates in the mind, but the effects show in the horse's actions through his body. Ray emphasized that it's in the mind. I began to see that when the mind is free, the obstacles blocking true willingness have been removed. Mentally, emotionally, and spiritually the horse is inspired by what he is experiencing. He accepts, allows, and is aligned with what is being offered or suggested. Mentally he is prepared, confident, and capable. A mind that is turned loose is artistic; it is akin to music or dance. It is felt from within and released. The benefits of turning loose for both horse and human (and frankly for every sentient being) are undeniable. I can say from deep within my heart that when horse and rider are free-spirited and united, there is a mystical elegance that releases and frees the souls of both.

And So It Is with Life

For me, turning loose means being willing. I feel the difference in my body when I am willing and inspired. A sense of willingness lends itself to an open mind and an open heart, and that openness is expressed through every cell. Free will is my most precious gift. It is where I find my passion, inspiration, and creativity. Responding to life from my true and free will fills me with energy. Body, mind, and spirit all seem to work together in harmony when I am living from an inspired will. In my life, the will has been the messenger of miracles.

Letting go of our acquired judgments, criticisms, and outdated thoughts can be tough. But once we experience the feeling that comes from believing in ourselves, we wonder how we could have waited so long. When I turn loose of my judgments and conditions, and my expectations and contradictions, I open my mind and find my natural cadence waiting there. Opening a closed mind unleashes the will, and the body naturally feels more at ease. Perfect practice takes practice; we have to begin from where we are.

Freeing the will is rarely accomplished by using the word *should*. *Should*, it seems, is counterintuitive to the will; it has a confining margin. All our shoulds seem to get in the way of our wants. One thing that tends to trigger my resistance is laundry. I just see it as an endless should. I want to ride my horse, but I should do laundry. What I have learned is that sometimes I can bargain with myself. I'll ride my horse first but then commit the rest of the day to catching up on chores. Or I'll say, "Just do these two things, then you can go ride." Often I end up doing a lot more than just two things on the list. The key for me is staying conscious in the process and not letting myself drift into self-pity or deprivation.

Life desires expression. This expression is free-willed when it is allowed rather than forced. Just as it is in nature or art, expression through an open mind can create masterpieces. Willingness is freedom, and freedom is the language of the soul. Life wants to move *through* our bodies, not *from* them.

Willingness is freedom, and freedom is the language of the soul.

Seeing the value of free will was important for me to learn with horses. But it also plays a role in all my life experiences. Allowing rather than forcing was crucial in writing this book. There were times I tried to write and the material just wasn't ready to come forth. It needed time to soak. To express myself authentically meant I had to allow the space and time required to gather my thoughts. I couldn't force my expressions and still have them be authentic. Each one of us is a unique expression of the will of creation, yet we tend to interrupt the dialogue through force.

Reward the Thought

We can learn to lighten up on ourselves and allow our ideas to surface. When we encourage experimentation, we open ourselves to new ways of living. The transition from force to will is allowed in the mind-set of acceptance. If we are willing to try something different, we may have to trust the process. There will be times we falter and times we fly. We don't have to, nor can we, get this all at once. It is a complete shift from what we were taught. Patience and compassion are pillars to an open, learning frame of mind.

Ray would often remind us to feel our horse's try. When we realize our horse is thinking about our request, right then we can release the pressure (or our cue) and encourage him that he is on the right track. Ray would emphasize this again and again. He wanted us to reward when the horse was thinking about it—before it happened! This builds curiosity and far outweighs any sense of "training" that is done through force. When it's the will of the horse, he fills in naturally. It will never be better than when it's the horse's idea. The horse can show us things we have never even imagined when we allow it to happen. Locked inside our own perceptions, we can see only a fraction of the picture. When we open our minds to the relationship, we find a whole new world waiting there.

By rewarding the thought, we applaud the horse's success, and he will try and try again. I really felt that Ray wanted us to give the success to the horse—to recognize all those overlooked times when the horse was trying, from just a thought to a complete change. We could start to see all those steps in between.

Recognizing the smallest things and applauding my horse's try made it interesting for both of us. And this early reward fed my horse's willingness. Ray's encouragement showed me the value in honoring the horse's try, and that was more valuable than any other attribute the horse had to offer.

Tapping into free will is a brilliant philosophy. In horsemanship there is scarcely a moment more fulfilling than when the mind of the horse is open and free. For that to happen, it takes a heightened level of trust. Horses are prey animals, and we are predators. To remove the barrier of fear can take a lifetime, but that one moment when the two minds meet as equals is a moment that is not soon forgotten. Ray had the ability to experience this more than most, and I believe this harmony is what he wanted us to know. He wanted this for the horses, and perhaps he wanted it for all life. Perhaps without really having thought of it in the big picture of our world, Ray demonstrated "the way" in his world—the world of horses.

The Integration of Heart and Mind: Letting Go of Habit

Willingness and mind can sometimes be conflicting. It is easy to see that willingness resides in the heart when the will wants to change what the mind wants to hold on to. Addiction is a habit that has become ineffective. Often it is ineffective because we are unconscious of the intrusion it presents to our willingness. Recognizing this is the beginning of channeling the will for our greatest intentions. To listen to and act on our will requires a deeper look into our self than the surface layer of mind and body. It takes a blend of thought and dedication to override such unconscious behavior. The best fuel for the fire of inspiration is willingness.

My true free will is always for my best interest. This is not to be confused with what I want. The wanting mind can and does become just the opposite of beneficial. It can launch us into striving for more and not accepting the present moment. My will is always present and does not require an outside source to fulfill it. My will is, in fact, who I am at the core. It is pretty easy to assume there may not be life on the planet without the will to live. The body is far too fragile to make it on its own. This light inside of us often goes unnoticed. We just put the car in drive and forget there is an engine. This metaphorical engine is fueled by our will. Yet so much of our focus is on the body and on thoughts. Living life from a merely physical perspective is like driving a car while looking at the steering wheel.

Addiction is a habit that has become ineffective. Often it is ineffective because we are unconscious of the intrusion it presents to our willingness.

I came from a family where alcohol was widely used. We used it to socialize, to cope, to play, and to feel larger than life. We also used it to overcome a lot of ineffective communication. Of course, in this case, the cure was worse than the disease. But drinking alcohol and using it as a cure for what ails you was a widely accepted practice in the era in which I grew up. Like so many others, I just assumed that was what everyone did to survive. I adopted it as my coping device. In my rebel childhood and adolescent years, I had a lot to cope with. Soon the habit of reaching for alcohol went south, into my unconscious mind, and quickly became an addiction.

It was 1996. I was living in the woods, on eighty acres, in a place called Bear Canyon. When I moved into this place, and into this time of my life, I was running. I was running fast and far. Life and my acquired stratagem had me buried in a circuit of chaos. I was strong and self-reliant, perhaps even on the edge of defiant. I needed no one, or so I thought. There was just one thing I did rely on heavily, my imagined escape through the use of alcohol.

One morning I startled awake, grabbing my chest. *Am I having a heart attack?* I wondered. All the thoughts came rushing in: *Do I need to call 911? Am I overreacting? I'm too young to die. The buzzards would find me before anyone would know I was missing.*

I had chosen this lifestyle. I liked my solitude. I got to choose my life. All those rules that separated me from the normal people didn't apply in the canyon. I was free but very alone. The sensation in my chest seemed to be subsiding. *Wow, I dodged another bullet.* I couldn't count the close calls I'd had in life. I felt as if I had a twelve-foot angel who stood by me through all my near misses. I used to say he worked overtime on my shift. This seemed to be another one of those moments when I just barely made it. I thanked him for rescuing me again. But what was it?

I had been experiencing some anxiety, obviously intense enough to raise my heart rate. I wasn't much of a crier, and I figured the panic I felt that morning had to do with burying a lot of my emotions concerning my father. He was reaching the end of his decade-long battle with cancer. In the grand scheme of things, I still harbored sorrows and regrets. There was so much I wanted to say, yet I never had the nerve. I feared when he died I would carry the burden of our past forever. Of course I loved my father, but I feared him more. He was a larger-than-life man who had two sides to him. You were either with him or without him. I had known both. My father and I were approaching the final stop on our journey, and I didn't feel ready. The hidden truth was that I was much more ready than I knew. In fact, I, too, was on the cusp of a monumental ending of my own.

If ever there was a time for answers to questions left unasked, it was then. Something was shaking me awake. At the time my way of prayer and meditation involved a practice I called journeying. I would sit quietly and allow my thoughts to settle. I also allowed freedom of expression, meaning images or messages came to me as if in a dream. I paid attention to these messages, and often they brought with them a much deeper understanding. In this quiet stance it seemed I transcended my intellect. I would have a conversation with my heart. I took great comfort in this practice. As I drifted far from the confines of my room and all the thoughts that plagued me, I listened for my answers. I cannot say where my mind was or for how long it had been away, but the message came loud and clear. As I opened my eyes and found myself once again in Bear Canyon, I spoke out loud the message I had received: "I must give up drinking." I couldn't believe I uttered the words. My first reaction was, *What if I fail?* I had tried to quit two other times, only to concede my will to my habit. I answered my own question as if from a higher self. I thought, *If I fail, then I am a drunk, and that is what I am now. I have nothing to lose. The only dishonor is in not trying.*

And so, I placed my sacred hawk feathers in my hair and wore a black suede dress. I gathered all the alcohol in the house and proceeded to the burn pile where I had been piling debris. It was quite a stash, including a half case of beer, a half gallon of vodka, and a box of wine. I also added to the pile a full carton of cigarettes. As I lit the fire, I asked that my father take this trait with him when he went. I felt I had inherited it from him unwillingly. Now my will was to return it from whence it came.

Just then a sweeping wind crept into the canyon from the south. With this gust, the smoke turned charcoal black. It moved away from me, following the switchbacks up the road. Twisting and turning in a slither, it took the shape of a black serpent.

Eerily I sensed a part of my history following the wind out of this place and out of my life. I can still feel the sense of divine intervention.

The willingness to let go of alcohol was also the willingness to be authentic. Shedding my dependency meant meeting life head-on. I had no idea that all along I had been preparing for this kind of release. The other two times I had given up alcohol were both short-lived reprieves. This time felt very different. This time it wasn't a "should." I realized I could never be truly free if I were dependent on escape for my deliverance. My free will called to me, and I happened to be listening. The signal was my fearful pain. On that fateful morning alone in the canyon, I was offered my true release and I took it. When the smoke cleared, I began a new life down a different path. I had made my choice, and I was willing.

My father died two days later.

The Narrow Gate

This is not the end of the story but the beginning. I have experienced great miracles in my life. Burrowed down within each one is the parental question, How bad do you want it? I feel that everyone has access to miracles. For me, the criterion to allow such a miracle was to first recognize it as such and then to act on the insights I received. I was bestowed a great gift indeed. However, this gift was not a get-out-of-jail-free card. I had some big choices to make. The transition into the unknown territory of sobriety was completely foreign to me. The ground was unstable beneath me. It was only the choice that was crystal clear, not the future.

I was with my father the night he died. It was late, after ten p.m., and his true love (my stepmother) asked me to go home.

My father's long journey was coming to a crossroads all his own. I cannot say how I knew, but I knew, and my stepmom knew too. Theirs was a love story of dedication. She had been by his side through it all. The final moments were theirs to experience. I agreed to go home and drove the thirty miles back to Bear Canyon in a daze. I have said of this kind of death that one can spend time, thought, and attention preparing for the one moment that cannot be prepared for. Every death is different, just as every relationship is different. The only thing I have experienced that is the same is that they are different. I got home feeling lost and confused. But a short time later, the phone rang, then the words… "It was a peaceful passing."

I returned to my father's house to spend my own time by his bedside and realized that this was not my father. If one thought permeated the mind, it was *Elvis has left the building*. I called my siblings, and by morning they all arrived. Not long after that, the coroner came. This was more than I could bear. I stepped outside on the deck. Their house was on a steep hillside, high in the trees. Outside with the morning birds, I could breathe again. There was too much to assimilate in the house—so many people, so many altered states, so much fear. I was suffocating. Thank goodness for this small window into nature's arms. She held me as she always has, like a mother with a child. I could hear the coroner's black van pull away, and I went back inside.

As I stepped into the room, there was my family standing in a circle, each with a brandy snifter in hand. It was time to toast my father in the manner he would have enjoyed—a good pull from the best booze in the house. This was my turning point. I stood on the cusp of past and future. There was a very narrow gate, and behind me was all I had ever known. On the outside of the gate and all around me was the comfort and security of the tribe, the culture and traditions. I belonged there. I had company; we even shared the same blood. Through the gate was the vast unknown. Through the gate was freedom. Just on the other side my will awaited. As they poured the amber liquid from the fancy bottle that held my fate, I panicked. *It's nearly to me*, I thought, holding the empty snifter. And right then, I looked down at the coffee table, and there was the cup of tea I had been drinking. I poured it in the glass. I smiled as I noticed it was the identical color of the booze. I stepped through the gate to my new life. The treasure I unburied on that misty morning in Bear Canyon would turn out to be my holy grail and the beginning of a reincarnated self. No less than the phoenix rising from the ashes, and much in the same way.

Willing to Grow

My sister battled life in depression and alcoholism. She watched as I transitioned out of our inheritance and found passion in living. She saw the life I built with my beloved horses in Bear Canyon. She knew I was happy, and she knew she wasn't. I know how desperately she wanted to find her own narrow gate. Once she asked me, "Did you find your passion when you found horses?" I answered, "No." Even they could not supply me with something that was buried so deep within me. I found my passion when I found my free will. I found my passion when I was willing to be who I was and accept life on life's terms. I found my passion when I found I had the will to choose my life. I "turned loose." I could meet all circumstance with a choice. I could live with heart.

That was decades ago. My heart has led me all the way from that gateway, full circle back to my own creations, back to my life. But this time it was and is authentically real. My life is every bit my own. Of course there are times still—quite often, in fact—that an old habit will seep through the cracks and find me in a vulnerable state. But never again has escapism been my choice. When one finds sanctity within, one is never without choice. Why then would we choose to leave our true heart's content, this place of solace? Why would we abandon what is real for what is false?

When one finds sanctity within, one is never without choice.
Why then would we choose to leave our true heart's content,
this place of solace? Why would we abandon what is real for
what is false?

The pain, the fear, the panic, and the doubt were bearers of gifts. I was not one to settle for such things, and my willingness held true. My willingness is at the root of these words I now write. Willingness is the means by which I grow and love and rise above the times of trouble and grief. Those times continue to pass through my life, like storm clouds on a winter's day. But they don't take up residency. They simply cannot linger beyond their designated time span. Only I can choose my heart's content, and each and every day I choose love. It is love that feeds my will. And it is my will to be free.

CHAPTER SIX

Inspired Action

L ONG AGO, AFTER I DIVORCED, I BOUGHT A TRAVEL trailer and lived as a bit of a wanderer. Back then I felt that if I had a house on wheels, all I would need was land. I moved from farm to farm. Still, my sense of security was elusive. I kept up my search for a place where I could lay some track to call my own. My true heart's content, or my deeper calling, was calling me home.

I was single and self-employed, and (other than the horses) all I owned could fit in that thirty-foot travel trailer. I was searching. There was a longing in my heart that had kindled since the latchkey kid found herself in the wandering animals. I was now in my early thirties. I had ridden down many of life's dead-end trails. Each time that I stumbled and fell, I gained more fuel for the dream that was my own.

My wanderings led me to my home in Bear Canyon. The land had a small, single-wide trailer. To me that was a bonus even though it was a run-down drug house. There was motor oil on the carpet in the living room where someone had rebuilt an engine. The entire place was in shambles. The land was as steep as a horse's face and overrun with weeds and Scotch broom. There were a couple of falling-down sheds that gave new meaning to the word *lean-to* and some chicken wire propped up by a two-by-four board over an old couch in the yard, making a coop. Obviously the place did not have curb appeal. What it did have was seclusion, and plenty of land to keep my horses. The run-down condition just meant I would have to work a little harder to create my vision. The price was right. The landlord was willing to negotiate the fees due to the condition of the house. I moved in just before winter.

I have a saying that I have adopted for those times when logic and passion are not necessarily on the same page: "Throw your hat over the fence." When you do, you're going to have to go get it. The richest learning experiences of my life have been when I tossed that hat! I spent five years in Bear Canyon building my dream of a horse setup. I saw it as the place I could finally settle down and dig in. Bear Canyon was a great place to start. It offered me the experience I needed, but it was only the beginning.

The Power of Pain

Pain is one of the most powerful motivators for change on the planet. Pain can be physical, emotional, mental, or spiritual. Pain pushes us to find new thought systems. I used my painful past to open my mind and reach beyond what I had never conceived. I became investigative and searched for freedom from my pain. I came to understand that the only power on earth that is more influential than pain is love.

When I first understood that I needed to adjust to fit a situation, I realized that concept pointed to the alchemy of change. When we do the same things over and over, we lose the mindfulness of our actions. Pain wakes us up. It was the power of pain that got my attention, not the circumstances. The powerful energy of pain can make us conscious of our deepest feelings. It can bring up everything from inspiration to resistance and back again. The power of pain teaches us to adjust. It is within the depths of it that we are often motivated to change our perceptions. Pain is often the catalyst that forces us to give to life what we have never given, and get from life what we have never had. I didn't realize at the time that my life in Bear Canyon was preparation for what came next. Commonly in great journeys, plans change and are redesigned countless times. As I grew up on an inner level, I grew out of my outer space. My pain had taught me well, and I was ready for the next phase of life.

Be Careful What You Ask For

Bear Canyon became a beautiful refuge. I tore down all the old buildings and built a barn, an outdoor arena, and a deck. I repaired the carport, making it a hay barn, and I cross-fenced pastures, cleared brush, and breathed new life into the house. I supplied the materials and did all the work. I was making a living an hour away, keeping alive a thriving business in Portland, Oregon. The satisfaction of building my dream inspired my actions…until the day the landlord raised the rent. In that moment I realized, indeed, this was not my own dream. I had built it for someone else. At any moment, another's actions could end it all. I came full circle back to the place of obscured security. Soon after this realization, I was repairing a fence by myself, and I was struggling in the hot sun. I looked up to the sky and said, "Dear Lord, let the next place be fenced." At that point I decided I wanted to buy land that no one could take from me. Once again, I found myself starting with nothing but my pride—and a little added experience.

Ray would say, "I can't teach experience." Experience teaches us. After five years of mistakes and accomplishments, I left my blood, sweat, and tears behind me. I decided that I would begin to gather information about how a single, self-employed female, with no credit and no savings, could buy land. I made an appointment with a mortgage broker. She subsequently told me of her friend who had twenty acres to sell—and he wanted to carry the contract. It seemed serendipitous, as the land was in a deep canyon and…the only thing on it was a fence. There was no power, water, or home—just a fence. I learned through this experience to be very specific. Even though it had a fence, it was broken-down barbed wire and had to be removed. Be careful what you ask for—you might just get it.

No Guarantees

When I bought "the land with one bad fence," there were no guarantees. I had no house or even confirmation of a building permit. I had no idea how I would pull it off. There were more uncertainties than opinions, and there were plenty of those! The key to success was this: I was absolutely inspired to own my own land. The notion erupted out of my mind with a power and force that was unstoppable by mere logic. When this kind of motivation occurs, we rise above the popular opinion of others and miracles happen.

Inspired action is when we remove the limitations that confine us. It is when life takes us for a ride rather than living a neatly managed life. We free the will, and the details follow. The most unbelievable, inconceivable, unimaginable things happen from this space. I was so thrilled at the opportunity to create a home that would be my "home at last" that I was willing to live in a tent. I was willing to forgo the comforts of the life that I knew to live my dream. Once I let go of the conditions, the conditions fell into place. Early in the planning stage, I received a call from a dear friend who said, "Mary, I wish you had some land, because we have this jobsite trailer we have to get rid of."

It was only the beginning of a long line of natural causes that brought my dream into reality.

Many of us get stuck in comfortable mediocrity. Too much routine stifles our growth. We can become stagnant for fear of change. Ray put no limits on his inspired action, and this was evident by his results. Whether it was his horse or another's, Ray committed his mind to the horse. I observed this commitment at a benefit clinic that he and his wife, Carolyn, hosted for their dear friend and mentor Tom Dorrance. The horse Ray was riding was reacting to the surroundings. Ray was helping the mare soften and find security with him. This seemed to be a great teaching opportunity and happened to arise right before the lunch break. A big photo shoot was scheduled at lunch, where all the clinicians who were part of this benefit would be photographed as a group. Carolyn had the challenge of keeping things moving as scheduled, and she told Ray of the time frame. Ray's focus was on helping his mare. It seemed she was more important to him than meeting deadlines. It all turned out well. The horse received the benefit of Ray's commitment. It wasn't long before he rode her peacefully out of the gate, and then he was available for an exceptional photograph.

Inspired action is when we remove the limitations that confine us.

I have seen this countless times in life: all too often we think we have to sacrifice a part of ourselves to have success when what we really must sacrifice is conformity. The greatest thinkers, the greatest athletes, and the greatest leaders of all time sacrificed conformity. Ray's life was original, and I wanted mine to be. He didn't have to sacrifice himself, and neither would I. I made the commitment and left my home in Bear Canyon to build my authentic world. And so far it's turned out to be wonderful!

The Trouble with Conformity

From a very early age, I didn't trust the norm. There was something about conformity that felt very unstable to me. I suppose my heart was such an active part of my perception that yielding it to someone else's opinion did not seem to be a viable option. I witnessed people giving up their lives in jobs they hated. I heard countless conversations that included sacrifice: "You must work hard and invest to be happy later." Working hard was never a problem for me, but working hard at something I hated seemed completely counterintuitive. I watched people lose their lives to shoulds and should-nots. It seemed the world was full of caverns of lost souls, created through conformity.

I know the look, in a horse or a human, when the world has had a numbing effect on the heart. Conformity can get us coming and going. When we take the world's opinion over our own, we're not seeing from a clear and personal perspective. We can start to question ourselves and then take on the outlook of others. Quite often what works for them doesn't quite fit for us, but we use it anyway. Relying on conformity is like taking advice from a disreputable source. We can assume too much when the masses congregate. Inspired action is sacrificed when we lose our deeper perspective. Trying to fit in can be a limiting action; it can confine us. We sometimes sell ourselves short in conformity. If we give up authenticity, we may look back on our life with a lot of regret and even wonder how we got here. We question our life, because, well, it really isn't our life we are living.

Fear perpetuates silencing the will. Through it all we may roll along in comfortable mediocrity, but still, there is something missing. What's missing is the opportunity to live the life we were meant to live. We can get to where we don't even recognize our own strengths anymore. We atrophy. There is an infinite will in us all that bears the question, Who am I really? This will, regardless of how concealed it is, is our true heart's content. It is inspired action waiting to be lived.

Inspired action comes from within our authentic consciousness. Ray Hunt was Ray Hunt. There will never be another like him because he was perfectly authentic. I see many clinicians, preachers, and teachers suggesting that other people be like them to do what they do. Sometimes this even translates to the hat they wear. Each individual horse (on any given day) is the teacher. I felt that that was what Tom was saying when he said, "If you go home and this doesn't fit, don't do it!" I am guessing Ray and Tom didn't want people emulating them—they wanted to build students, not future clinicians. From what I could see, they were pointing to the horse as the teacher, not to themselves. When we make an idol out of someone, the shift in focus causes us to lose track of the ideal.

Conformity does have its usefulness. It can lead us to the start of our own awakening, if we utilize it. Ray was a master at seeing the effectiveness in using conformity to gain interdependence. He nurtured the horse's natural instinct to belong while also honoring his self-preservation. He said, "I want them to do my thing their way." This is it—a fabulous example of how to be *on* this earth but not *of* it. Ray worked the line between mind and heart. When we learn to do what this world asks of us authentically, we do "their thing" our way. Freedom is what's important to a conscious being—freedom to *be*. Authenticity is what feeds our sense of freedom.

My life changed dramatically when I trusted my will instead of following my fear. When I moved away from Bear Canyon,

I left behind the paradigms I had acquired from the world as I grew. I believed in myself, and I was willing to see the habits that kept me from the life I truly wanted. As I walked away from alcohol, cigarettes, and regrets, I walked into a brand-new world. A world I created from love, not from fear. I began letting go of fears about money. It seemed there was always just enough. My motto was "I do what I love, and the bills get paid," and it was completely true. It seemed that when I committed to my life, life became my ally. Gifts started showing up just when I needed them, from a roll of fencing to the house I lived in. My willingness opened the gate for my success. This was just the beginning of learning about life. I had to first learn the importance of unlearning what the opinions of the world had taught me. I cleaned the slate for a fresh new start and wasn't afraid to take it.

Freedom is what's important to a conscious being—freedom to be. Authenticity is what feeds our sense of freedom.

The Leading Edge

The tip of an aircraft wing contacting the air is called the leading edge. Our personal leading edge is our initial contact with the world. It says a lot about how we feel about ourselves. Are we true to ourselves, or do we project what we think people want? My capacity for intimacy with life determines the direction I take in the world. Inspired action is our true, authentic course. I once said, if we were all transparent (so that everyone could see into our thoughts), wouldn't we be more selective of the thoughts we claim as our own? The leading edge is our point of connection with the world at large.

I remember when I was a young woman my father would call me on the phone. One day during a conversation, I noticed that my voice changed dramatically while I was talking to him; I actually shape-shifted in his presence. I realized in that moment that I had spent my life trying to be a daughter worthy of his love. This "trying to be" conditioned me to be someone other than who I am.

Many years later, after my father's death, I realized how very sad it was for us both that I had been afraid to be authentic. I began seeing a counselor, and shortly thereafter my mother also passed away. This was an eye-opening time in my life. I was no one's daughter. By then I had done a lot of personal reflection and had years of practice being more authentic. My counselor suggested I write my father a letter. Even though he had long since passed, it would be a way of clearing the slate. The letter would be my voice telling my father who I really am and how I wanted him to see me. In that letter I said, "I am so sorry I never let you know me."

The relationship between father and daughter is a stimulant for emotion. This primordial bond can deeply impact every other relationship we have. When I became aware that I had unconsciously altered who I was around my father, I realized I felt very insecure. Inspiration and insecurity do not coexist. I felt my heart open as I recognized this unconscious habit. That significant obstacle, once recognized, produced an opening to my freedom.

Once, at a Tom Dorrance clinic, I heard a gal say, "My horse doesn't like to be with the other horses, and he can't stand to be away from them either." How many times do we feel this kind of conflict within ourselves? We search for approval from others, yet often this approval is loaded. It is loaded because, if it's given, it can be taken away. Seeking approval actually gets in the way of our own acceptance. Relying on outside circumstances provokes insecurity. We can feel unsafe, both alone and with others.

Just like we can't make a horse *feel* secure, we have to introduce him to his own sense of security. Learning security for ourselves inspires our own consistent sense of well-being.

Perfect practice is realizing that who we are at our core is worth knowing. The leading edge is allowing our introduction to others to be both authentic and comfortable. Ray taught us to be very aware of how we approach a horse. Our approach can often make or break our success. If we come storming up to a horse without any understanding, we're apt to be met with quite a lot of resistance. It's that way with a lot of things in life. In working with horses there is a term called desensitizing. People use the process of exposing the horse to many unusual things so that the horse will gain confidence. But often people do too much exposing. They overexpose and then create the very thing they don't want, which is fear. Being authentic does not mean overexposing those around us to who we are. It means allowing our capacity for comfortable honesty to surface and expand. In the same way that it's best to read a horse's signals, we can also learn to be sensitive to the receptivity of others. Finesse in relationships is an art—it's easy to do too little or too much. I was assuming the worst from my father. I assumed he wouldn't love me just the way I was. This was an unconscious opinion I held from childhood. I was preventing a real relationship with my father based on the fear of his disapproval. I set myself up for failure. This was a strong fear-based habit that kept me from loving and being loved. Perfecting the leading edge is perfecting a communicative balance.

The Art of Exposure: Learning Acceptance

I once worked with a big thoroughbred horse. The previous owner had tried to expose him to potentially frightening things, thinking he would overcome fear that way. They had a plastic bag full of pop cans and thought, if they exposed the horse to it, he would learn to accept rattling and clanking. It was a tormenting experience for the horse. The people did not gauge his level of fear, nor did they offer him release from it. They tied the bag of cans to the saddle and ran him around the arena. This horse did the only thing he knew to do; he tried to escape. He was so frightened that he attempted to jump through the mirrors at the end of the arena. These folks did not intend to hurt the horse; they had not yet learned the fine art of exposure.

Being authentic does not mean overexposing those around us to who we are. It means allowing our capacity for comfortable honesty to surface and expand.

The art of exposure includes all the degrees between acceptance and fear. Balance is essential to well-being. The tin cans created so much emotional and physical pressure that the horse had to escape. Understanding conditions and expanding the capacity to tolerate them are what the art of exposure is. The ability to take off the pressure, before fear sets in, can make the difference between disaster and success. Positive exposure would have saved that horse from a traumatic encounter. I know this is a real art in human relationships too. Release from pressure, given to someone who feels overwhelmed, can actually draw that person to us for security. Continued pressure can and does create just the opposite effect. If fear shows up in our relations, and communication ends in fear, then we know we've overexposed ourselves or others.

Ray would say, "Know when you're well-off." This held so much wisdom for me, everything from being in the moment to counting your blessings and knowing when to quit. Each piece of wisdom offers a unique attribute toward perfect practice. Knowing when to quit can sometimes be a great challenge. We have all seen famous athletes who had unbelievable success; they may have reached the top of their game countless times. There is a pivotal moment when stepping down would leave them with lasting success. They would forever know they had achieved greatness. All too often, fame (or other factors) drives these great athletes to continue to strive. After years of an illustrious career, they plummet. These natural achievers leave their brilliant career in failure and then carry that failure forward. It does not mean they were wrong, nor does it take away from their achievements. It just means that the last thing they remember is the pain of defeat. This easily sets up the future for more of the same. To know when you're well-off is to know acceptance and to learn to end on a good note.

The art of exposure is to tune into your own natural cadence and that of the world. Inspired action has a dynamic flow. It is interactive. No one else can offer to this world what is uniquely our own. Learning to work with my environment (rather than bracing against it) offered a vitality to the sensation of success.

I found that the world at large, with its aching desire for more, undermined my natural inspiration. Diminished inspiration was the result of constantly seeking procurement. We learn greed; we do not inherit it. The belief that if something is good, then more must be better is not natural—it is fundamentally flawed. When I tuned into the rhythm of fulfillment, I saw that joy came from the flow of passion, not necessarily from the results. I began to recognize perfection because I sensed it. Balance and well-being, peace and joy, bliss and all the sensations of contentment are of my inner being. I didn't have to acquire these sensations. They exist within me. Once I allowed myself to really experience the fulfillment of inspiration, I understood a different kind of success. It was internal. Seeing inspiration at the heart of it all, I enjoyed the process a lot more. I didn't need to strive for more. I was happy at each stage. I found I could simply enjoy these wonderful, natural attributes that I was allowing.

My horse Poco has seen a lot of miles in a painful past. I am only beginning to understand how he feels—just scratching at the surface of his buried emotions. For the first two years that I had him, I focused on what we did rather than how he felt.

I am fortunate. I have no shortage of desire when it comes to learning about the horses I love. I am inspired to learn from them, and this keeps me coming back for more. The main thing that sets me back is unconsciousness. After decades of riding, it is easy to take the little things for granted. I am humbled by my mistakes. These mistakes come when I forget who it is that I am riding. Horses are highly intelligent animals, and they will remind us when we have let our egos get in the way of our relationship. Understanding my horse meant I had to remain conscious. Poco told me more than once to pay attention. Eventually I had to listen.

Like any other discipline, there are models for riding horses. With these models come patterns of thinking. I find that I compromise my awareness when I am in a routine. Walk, trot, and canter are riding standards that come to mind. I would get on, warm up the horse, go around the rail, pick up a trot, then do some circles and perhaps lope. For many years I believed this was a good way to start my rides. That was until I bought my horse Poco. He was the first horse I had that really didn't like this model of thinking. Perhaps other horses had tried to tell me about the trouble. But Poco was the one who wouldn't have it any other way. His resistance to it was just too volatile for him to stay passive. He would do what I asked, though I always sensed that he wished he was somewhere else. All the horses I had before Poco seemed to enjoy the simplistic, predictable agenda.

Before I had Poco, his experience with people involved a lot of pain. He had not yet gained trust in humans. In fact, he had lost any of the natural trust that he may have had. The horses I had raised trusted me. They never knew any other way. I actually became a source of security to them. But Poco was lost and scared and required much deeper attention than I was giving him. Unfortunately, due to my patterns, I underestimated his feelings.

I noticed he would shy in certain places in the arena, and I just wrote it off as no big deal. There were many times Poco would explode after saddling. As I led him away from the tack room, he would jump straight up in the air. I wondered about these things but didn't take them seriously. He even bucked me off at a clinic, but I blamed it on overreacting in a new environment. I kept justifying his behavior rather than taking his feelings seriously. That was until the day he finally told me, in no uncertain terms, to listen.

I was in my regular routine, the pattern of walk, trot, and canter. Poco shied away from the wall in his usual spot, and I put him back on the line and kept going. We rounded the next corner of the arena, and as we headed down the long wall, my toe tapped the plywood siding. That started him bucking. In his first jump, he folded nearly in half. I rode it out, and then he launched toward the center of the arena and jumped again. I rode that jump too, and with that he shied and twisted and jumped a third time. This time I lost my balance and sailed off his back like a lawn dart. I hit the clay-packed soil on my ribs. The next thing I knew, I was on my hands and knees gasping for even one full breath of air. Then I got on and put him right back into the walk, trot, and canter pattern, the one that had gotten me in this mess to begin with. Within minutes the adrenaline wore off and I realized I was pretty badly hurt. I stepped down and limped away like a battered combatant.

I felt a rush of emotions fill the empty cavern of my forgotten senses. I felt a wave of guilt. I could hear a voice in my head saying, *You left him.* In that moment I realized I had left him long before I even started. I had never really seen Poco in the first place. I was riding him like I would any other horse. I saw only what was on the surface. I saw him as a horse, not as an individual. I put him in a box. Poco and I had a lot in common. I didn't like being boxed in, and neither did he. This was the beginning of a real relationship with Poco. I would start over, and this time I would be very conscious. I knew I had to pay close attention to all the little things that I had previously taken for granted. Pain is my teacher. Coming off Poco made me realize I had a lot to learn, and he was just the horse to teach me.

I got bucked off because I was focusing too much on what to do—and not really grasping what was motivating the doings. You might say I lacked empathy. I had ample empathy in general, but this particular horse required a much more in-depth understanding than any other horse I have had. I didn't recognize his depth because on the surface he was very, very still. You know what they say about still water. This horse is brilliant. He is not a machine. He is a complex thinker, and his pain runs deep. I now believe his levelheaded mind was all he could use to survive the amount of trauma he endured. He just shut down and checked out. But when he came to his senses, he had a lot to say. When I scratched that surface layer and asked Poco his opinion, his fear was allowed to be expressed.

Both Poco and I had a lot at stake. I wanted the best relationship I could have with him. As I have said, the relationship with my horse is a mirror for the relationship I have with life.

One night while working with Poco in the arena, I just paused. In that moment I reflected on Ray saying, "Know when you're well-off." I wondered if he wasn't really teaching the ultimate course in acceptance. In the past, if Poco would shy at the corner of the arena, I would do things that I thought might help him get over his fear. The key word here is *do*. I tried this and that, but what I hadn't tried was acceptance. I never just paused and gave him time to sort it out. This evening I just paused and rubbed his neck. I let him work through his thoughts. I didn't ask him to do anything. As I did this, I rode ahead a step or two, but I didn't insist. I gave him an option. He didn't have to be in that spot in the arena. The best way I can describe this change of heart in me is empathy. I stopped thinking he should be different than he was. I felt a real deep sense of compassion for him. Soon Poco learned to trust. And this was the greatest success for us both. The walk, trot, and canter pattern is nothing without sincere unwavering trust.

The leading edge of inspired action is a blend of authenticity, compassion, and acceptance. These attributes together form the basis of authentic relationships.

Now, when I work with Poco, I am much more tuned in to what is happening for him and for me in the present moment. I am letting go of wanting more, and focusing on where we both are today. Words cannot express the sensations I now experience. It is as real as the wisdom Ray and Tom offered. It is not something I learned. It is something I have tapped into. Now I can see that when my horse gives me his trust, his mind, and his heart, we are both learning acceptance. By really focusing on how my horses react in each step, from saddling to walking off, I know them much better. I now have a much clearer understanding of their emotions, from self-preservation to security, and I am honoring the same in myself. I realize that when I really care about how they feel, I have a real and unified relationship with them. Less is more. Trust does not happen all at once. It is a process, and it grows deeper with each success.

The leading edge of inspired action is a blend of authenticity, compassion, and acceptance. These attributes together form the basis of authentic relationships. Outgrowing our dependence on conformity frees our individuality. I begin to see that my pain has purpose. It fosters growth and matures me. And the fact that there are no guarantees is actually a blessing. It means that our options and potential are limitless. Inspired action is how we express our unique purpose and relate to the world.

Chapter Seven

Experience

P ARKING MY TOES UNDER MY DOG, I WARM MYSELF
from the morning's chill. My heart settles in, and I think,
Home at last. I have just returned from a long trip up
north. Long to me is ten days, so that may be a relative statement.
Going to faraway places opened my mind and my senses to so
much more imagery and experience. I saw roadside cafés with
blackberry pies and deep harbor marinas cradling lavish yachts.
I toured the open sea where orcas breached and salmon jumped
in a melody of blue and silver. I saw purple sunsets and rusty,
old steam engines. I saw the wealthy and the poor sharing an
island. I saw a world I had never seen before. I brought it home
in my mind through my senses, yes, but I brought it back in my
heart through my experience.

Ray Hunt worked with hundreds of horses a year and
traveled thousands of miles. He filled his life with experience.
Experience is the sustenance of life, and the more we are willing
to absorb, the more we fill in the details of our life's journey. Ray's
life was vast yet focused. He had a deep, undeniable purpose,
and that is where he put his full attention. We all have varying
capacities of focus—from multitasking to monotasking. We
have our genre. Ray's heart, soul, and mind were focused on
bringing a better deal to the horse. Ray shared with us that he
felt he owed it to the horse. As he came to understand there was
a better way to work with horses, he began giving back what he

felt he had missed in those early years, before he met Tom. Ray was always a great horseman, but once he found out (through his experience) how fulfilling the partnership he so cherished could be, he became driven.

Ray was not alone on this journey. He had a partner in life who completely supported his devotion—his wife, Carolyn. She covered the same miles and ate the same dust. She was there from sunup to lights out, never wavering from the cause, always supporting from the sidelines. Carolyn handled all the many details, from public relations to laundering the dusty clothes. Ray and Carolyn spent their lives and the bulk of their experiences on the road. Once I asked her, "It is clear that Ray Hunt's passion is the horse. What's yours, Carolyn?" She replied simply, "Ray Hunt." I watched her devotion like I watched Ray's hands on his reins—with my whole heart. I knew this was not any old marriage I was witnessing. I have always said, "You're as healthy as your partner." Carolyn's dedication to Ray could only be as unconditional as Ray's dedication to the horse, or it couldn't have lasted. The display of both (for me) was a once-in-a-lifetime education in devotion.

Devoted experience does not have to include thousands of miles, hundreds of horses, or even being in a committed relationship. Devotion can be a solitary experience. Being alone can even enrich a life experience. I found this to be true as I devoted some time to deepening my own awareness. I could acutely tune into the messages life sent me by keenly intuiting each experience I was in. Alone, I could interpret my own unique, heartfelt message. How I felt, what I saw, and how I understood my experience would offer either wealth or poverty of the mind. I was deeply devoted to understanding life on life's terms, and for many years I did this alone.

One of the ways I found to deepen my awareness was simple but effective. I chose a random section of ground on my land where I would spend frequent blocks of time. It was on a steep hill, not far from my house. The spot was about four feet wide and equally long under a small maple tree. The first time I visited it, I sat on the ground. It was hard as clay. It really wouldn't have mattered too much where I sat, how I sat, or what I sat on. The experiment was about experiencing one consistent location in many varied states. I chose being in nature. That is where I am at home. Being there, it was easy for me to focus my attention. But some people might choose a city sidewalk or a crowded mall. The spot might be a church or a marketplace. The important element was to experience the same, very specific location in many states of mind and body, in nighttime and morning, fall and summer, cold and heat, tired and inspired. I became acutely aware of my reactions and perceptions. The outside environment offered me a window into myself. All of me surfaced there, doubts and confidence, love and fear. It broke me of thinking the world caused my feelings. My feelings showed their true colors without cause. I simply witnessed my responses to all that is.

I noticed countless variations of perceptions and feelings, aches and pains, fears and pleasures. Common responses as well as surprising ones rose to the surface. I experienced perfect weather and harsh cold. It was as if I could live all perceptions without leaving the spot. I returned to my spot over and over. I went in winter, summer, fall, and spring; I sat with the birds, the ants, rain, and clouds. This four-by-four place offered discomfort and peace, as well as anxiety and inspiration. I witnessed emotions from boredom to confusion and a myriad of others. All this was experienced on one piece of ground no bigger than my kitchen table.

I returned to my spot simply for the awareness of the changing experience. It was an experiment in realizing how I could open my mind to the vast plain of life in a single moment, on a very small scale. Life is what lives through me. It is not what I do or where I do it. It's how I feel and what I learn. My life is not a specific incident, role, or place. I am not the labels my mind puts on things. I am living a life, and that is expressed through my attention, hope, focus, and sorrow. Life is moving and changing. It's wandering through daylight and nightfall, through old dogs and purring kittens. The endlessness of experience is what life is about for me. The stage is set. I can choose my roles.

Life is what lives through me. It is not what I do or where I do it. It's how I feel and what I learn.

Life easily takes place without our navigation. How often do we find ourselves on autopilot? We wander into the kitchen, grab the same coffee cup, "our favorite," and we walk across the floor to the same chair, cloaked with our favorite blanket. How much life do we miss, seeing the same way we did yesterday? The world changes constantly, yet we easily remain stagnant in our thoughts and perceptions. I found great value in opening to a new outlook each morning and laying to rest my old ones at night. I hold dearly in my heart the precious wealth of imagery I acquire throughout the day, discarding those images I would not choose as my own. My thoughts about my experiences build my future. In that space, I developed a practice of selective thinking, releasing ineffective or outdated thoughts to open the space for fresh new ideas. It feels liberating to know that I have thoughts; my thoughts don't have me.

Experiences open our minds, and it is no different for horses. Expanding their world and deepening their awareness enriches the lives of horses too. It can be a bit routine and boring standing in a field all day. It can even be demoralizing for the horses that must live in a box stall. Horses want to experience life too. They have incredible minds, and each horse is different. They have varying personalities, interests, and abilities. I have seen first-hand how deepening a horse's experience inspires him to learn.

Build a Fence with Him

Almost twenty years ago, at a Tom Dorrance clinic, one of my friends was riding a young stallion in a horsemanship class. I had a lot of respect for this man. I had met him a few years before, when I bought a mustang from him. He was really good with horses, and Kiger Mustangs were his horse of choice. He worked with the real Kigers, not the "breed" born in captivity. These horses lived in the Steens Mountain Wilderness of Oregon. They were named for where they lived, in one of the most rugged places in the state, the Kiger Gorge. This man believed in his horses, and it showed.

At the time of the clinic, Far Go was a colt and just weaned from his mother. I wanted to be a source of support and security for him, but Far Go wasn't having anything to do with me. I asked my friend if he had a suggestion for me. Of course he was not at this clinic as a teacher but as a student. I often wonder why I asked him rather than Tom. I suppose it was a comfort factor for me, but the point is in the answer he gave. He just smiled and said, "Build a fence with him," and rode away. Well, my young pride was pretty fresh, so I wasn't going to chase him down and ask him to explain. But I did think about the statement, and I have quoted it many times since then.

When I got back home, I went out and got Far Go and wondered what this fella could have meant. I didn't have a fence to build right then, but I did have some irrigation to move, so I brought the colt along. As I dragged the long, heavy hose across the grass, there were ample opportunities for this young horse and me to unite. I had named him Far Go for inspiration. Far Go was the same age as my sobriety. I had gotten him when he was two months old and I was two months sober. I always saw us, in a sense, growing up together. My world was brand new back then, and Far Go had also just been born into an ever-changing environment.

When Far Go was separated from his mother, he really struggled. I felt sadness and empathized with his loss. It was as if his heart hardened. I remember as a young girl feeling the same way when my parents divorced. My mother went to work, and I started rebelling. I can't say what was going on for Far Go, but I saw an innocence start to fade in him. He'd lost his God-given security, and I was no substitute. I moved him to a pasture with my mare Cayenne, but she did not offer the nurturing his mother had. I feared his innocence was lost forever, and I felt responsible. This shift was not something anyone could explain—it was inside Far Go, and I could see it. I wanted to bring his young heart back to the surface again. But I was going to have to be creative to do that.

I began to use our experiences to set up situations where Far Go could look to me for support and guidance. I knew I would never be able to offer all that Far Go needed, but by building confidence together, perhaps we would build a bond. I took Far Go when I checked the oil in the ole pickup, and then sometimes the whole family—dogs, cats, goat, Far Go, and I—would just walk the half-mile driveway to the end of the road. We just set out to see the world together. I eventually figured out how I could do a lot of things with a colt on a rope. And Far Go learned how to build confidence. The experiences we had together taught us both, and we were better off for them.

"Build a fence with him" became code for "mix it up," "get creative," or "just live!" It wasn't what we were doing together; it was more about how we succeeded in what we were doing. Our ongoing interaction with many various experiences gave Far Go and me a strong relationship. We weren't limited to the round corral for our education. "Build a fence with him" broadened the scope and took the agenda out of the so-called training process. The only purpose was to grow our partnership through the combined experience. Far Go and I have learned together for well over twenty years now. I consider him my lifelong partner, and I feel certain he feels the same about me. We did grow up together during those early years. We learned to stay together through good times and bad. Living all the nuances of life together builds a lasting bond that only grows stronger.

Empirical Knowledge

Horses learn through their experience. We would do well to understand this attribute. Experiential lessons offer empirical knowledge, or knowledge gained by experience. I have said, "You can't learn to ride a horse from reading a book." There comes a time when you have to get on. Empirical knowledge (for better or worse) is not easily forgotten.

Once fear is learned in a horse or a person, it easily gets reinvested over and over. Sometimes horses carry that fear with them for the rest of their lives. People can consciously work through fear if they can become aware of it. But horses rely on a consistent, improved experience to unlearn fear. Even then it can be so ingrained that it's buried too deep to recover. When left unattended, unconscious fearful thoughts repeat until fear overshadows truth. Unless we can improve on our thoughts, unconscious historical fear becomes the knowledge we rely on. Fear starts influencing our experiences. And it is in our experiences that relationships grow or die. Whether it is a marriage, a job, a child, a dog, a Sunday sermon, or a Sunday drive, how we experience our world will determine that relationship's future.

When left unattended, unconscious fearful thoughts repeat until fear overshadows truth.

Empirical knowledge is how the world matures. No one knew how to fly before flight was developed. They had to experiment. For that matter, computers, telephones, cars, and the entire progression of all life on the planet have expanded through empirical knowledge. This explains how experience can be the elixir for life.

Have you ever noticed that when one thing goes wrong, it can start a chain reaction of misfortune? As frustration builds momentum, it can seem as if we're caught up in a gill net of disaster. Every direction seems hazardous. It is often at this point that people just cave in, though this can be the moment when we are closest to freedom. Each time we are caught in a gill net of misfortune, we have a choice to fight or surrender. If we fight, we only get more ensnarled in the ropes of our defensiveness. When we surrender, we can open our minds and allow new experiences to drift in. We can actually recognize the light at the surface and realize that there is another way. If we think in terms of fight or die, we can lose all hope. When we can free our mind from our hazardous thoughts, new opportunities appear. I find this is very difficult to do when I am defensive. So my first step is to surrender.

Work Ethic

Ray Hunt worked with horses for a living. He worked on ranches. He didn't learn his craft because he set out to get a diploma in horsemanship. He learned it because he had to use it. He mastered it because it inspired him. His experience led him to his purpose. When working with horses for a living, there is a job to do. Ray found that a work ethic was important not only to him but also to the horse. He would say of the horse, "The first day he will cost you money, the second day he holds his own, and the third day he's on the payroll." All too often we keep our horses in a box; that box is usually an arena or a corral. But it's a metaphorical box that we place ourselves in. Experience feeds us purpose. We don't have to try to recruit our passion. We can go out and expose ourselves to options. So often people (and horses) become bored with life—"the same old, same old." The experience elixir is the potion of motion. Drink life in and get on the payroll.

I remember hearing Ray talk about the Olympics. His eyes shone with respect and admiration for the athletes he observed. He spoke about the level of experience they must have to reach that standard of greatness. I have thought of this many times. If I ride my horse for an hour a week, I am really limiting our experience. Olympic athletes live, drink, and breathe their craft. They are up and in the practice arena while the rest of us are still in a dream world. The reward is equal to the investment. We can't broaden our scope while limiting our experience.

How much do we expect of ourselves, our horses, or our loved ones, with very limited investment of experience? I often say to folks, "Where would you have learned anything else?" Unless we experience a different course of action, we will follow the ant trail. If we want enriching lives, it may be that we have to look up and out and chart a different course. If our jobs are taxing and we limit the experience to simply making money, then a paycheck is all we get. And if a paycheck is all we get, then once cashed, we're broke again. This is how we experience emotional poverty. Once someone said to me, "I wish I would win the lottery." I asked what they would experience if they did. The wealth we seek is in our experience. The money isn't the wealth; the experience is. We can enrich our lives at every turn when we embrace our life experience.

Sentience

The relationship I witnessed between Ray Hunt and the horse seemed to be seamless. I did not see the same flow with Ray and people. The challenge to convey the depth of what he taught had to be insurmountable at times. He openly shared that he couldn't teach this way of seeing the horse, but he could try to make us aware of it. Ray looked for ways of getting people to recognize a new experience and digest it. But he couldn't learn it for them. The realization of Ray's intention was met with the individual's filter. The same is true with religion and philosophy. We must each interpret the teaching. Our expression of Ray's wisdom is as unique as the horses we ride. This is why it is not a technique; it is a philosophy. This is also why it's lasting and real. It is a way of seeing, not a way of doing. Teaching this is a tall challenge.

Ray would illustrate a series of examples and link them together to point to the potential in the partnership between horse and human. No one can teach potential, but great teachers can get you to look for it. Results were not the principle of the teaching; they came through the experience. Ray's clinics were not a classroom; they were a workshop. Ray offered an unending commitment to epitomize sentience and awareness.

How does one write a textbook on sensations of the heart when every moment changes? I can't imagine the depth of thought that went into Ray's investment. He was faced with setting up the right experiences so as to offer people elevated vision. He shared the recognition that his own teacher Tom had had the same dilemma when introducing this philosophy to him. Tom offered Ray the experiences that got him to reach beyond what he already knew. Ray would share, "It's amazing what you can learn when you think you know it all." Ray set out to offer the world what he had realized for himself, and his lifework was set in motion.

Ray's enigma was to awaken mankind's awareness. This is a challenge that sages throughout time have confronted. Ray's stage happened to include the partnership he knew to be real—that of man and horse. From what I observed, it wasn't so much of a "how" that he was teaching as a "when." The sentient moment is now. The leading edge in the relationship when horse and man meet is not a consistent factor; it is a variable. The awareness of the sentience in that moment brings the consistency into it, and this is the first principle I gained from the *experience* of Ray Hunt.

Looking back, I see the intense challenge of the curriculum. I wonder if the challenge was why, at times, questions seemed to be exasperating for Ray. He knew what he wanted to convey, yet the leading edge was constantly changing. And all too often, although people came there to learn, they did not yet have the capacity for the knowledge. I suppose it would be a little like teaching a class in a foreign country in whose language you didn't speak. Ray knew what he wanted to offer, though I'm guessing he didn't always know how to translate it on a level of the individual's awareness. What teacher can reach every student? There was only one Ray Hunt, yet many people and horses came to him. I can see that varying degrees of skills and experience could create a great teaching challenge. I don't know many people who could have initiated such a dramatic change in an intensely traditional methodology.

I sense that this challenge could be why Ray stuck so closely to absolute basic practice. The experiences he gave to riders were consistently simple, and yet they offered a heightened awareness of the horse. Not everyone was able to comprehend all of what they were absorbing while they were there, but there was no doubt of the mastery in the lessons. I wondered if that's why Ray kept the lessons simplistic. Perhaps the basic principles allowed the riders to feel as well as think about the lessons. Sometimes overthinking can get in the way of learning. In this way, Ray was a master teacher, offering the same experience to all while accepting a myriad of comprehension in his students.

Ray's style of teaching was a creative analogy for living an imaginative life. I allowed experiences to open my perspective rather than closing down my mind. With an open mind I recovered my natural potential for learning. The style of learning I experienced in school involved a learning curve where my individuality was lost to the performance. Old-school teaching was where I learned to sacrifice wisdom for the effect, my heart for the grade. Ray Hunt offered a new way to learn.

Experience is the wealth of our life. Perfect practice is embracing each experience with a child's mind. A mind that is inquisitive and reverent and born from an open heart.

Experience can be bridleless or constrained, awe inspiring or monochromatic. We can launch long-held desires or procure forged-in-steel fears. Experience makes the difference in how we see, taste, touch, and smell. All our senses are led by our particular experiences. The scent of a campfire reunites me with warmth and fun, while cooking artichokes reminds me of when I was a child and got terribly ill from dipping them in soured mayonnaise. Many people love artichokes. I did before I had a bad experience. Our experiences are uniquely our own. As I write, an early fall rain hits the dusty soil to create the smell of autumn. I flash back to other autumns when I wrote essays and journals. Writing and autumn go together.

We are given an endless journey through our experiences. Some we wouldn't choose, and others we wouldn't lose. Experience is the wealth of our life. Perfect practice is embracing each experience with a child's mind. A mind that is inquisitive and reverent and born from an open heart. When we are born and begin to take in our surroundings, we have no preconceptions. We are honest and express our experiences naturally. As we come full circle in this life, we can learn to revisit this quality and welcome the gift of our experience.

CHAPTER EIGHT

Learning Trust, Gaining Confidence

P OCO IS AN EXTREMELY KIND AND GENTLE HORSE. I had bought him for my husband to ride. At the time he seemed safe enough. But I came to realize Poco is an introvert. He had been through hell in his life and kept it all to himself. I might have been the first person to ask Poco his opinion about things. When we met, we began developing open communication. I offered Poco choices rather than forcing my will. As our relationship developed and he felt more secure, he began to express some of the resistance that he had stored up for years. I have found, through this and other experiences, that sometimes introverts actually have the most to say.

I was caught off guard when Poco finally decided to demonstrate his fear and resistance and bucked halfway across the arena. But that conversation is the one that changed our relationship for the better. And in turn the understanding that came with it expanded my awareness and improved my horsemanship, but not before I lost my confidence. I was humbled by the pain of the experience. Falling off a horse can really hurt physically. Fortunately, for the most part, the body heals pretty quickly. But that is only part of the healing. What this kind of injury can do to the mind and to one's confidence can be much more complex to overcome.

I tend to lack confidence in a relationship with a horse (or a person) when it's not authentic. I like to know the feelings of people and horses I come in contact with. I realize that actions typically stem from feelings. Of course authenticity isn't always the case in relationships. Reactions and fear, personalities and perceptions are all variable within each individual.

My crucial mistake with Poco was being unaware of the cause of his tension. If I don't know the cause, it's pretty hard to get to the cure. It was essential that I start over. Poco and I both had a lot of fear to let go of and a lot to unlearn. With horses or in life, we can all get along pretty well with what we know, until the day we hit what seems to be a proverbial wall. When life sets up a challenge that feels unmanageable, we are faced with those three options again: change it, accept it, or leave it. I had no intention of leaving this horse. He had become a good friend, and we considered him part of the family. With that in mind, I also couldn't accept that he would explode without notice. So this meant I was going to need to do things differently. Little did I know how much I would come to understand about relationships, fear, and life in the process. I would have to expand my knowledge of how to help Poco while at the same time honor my own survival. I hadn't dealt with this level of fear in a horse before, at least not in an introverted horse. Poco, with his perfect blend of kindness, intelligence, and fear, ultimately brought me to my shortcomings and gave me the motivation to become a better person. He did this by teaching me the true meaning of trust.

To unlearn fear requires a much deeper look into the subject of trust and confidence. Humans' dependency on trusting outside circumstances in order to have confidence can be counterproductive. In life there are times of unity and times of trouble. Trust and confidence lend themselves as a learning process, not as a final conclusion. In other words, when we explore our levels of fear and observe the circumstances, we can see that there are many variables. If I simply trust something because it has worked in the past, I often miss seeing the contributing factors. When I learned to understand the circumstances surrounding fear, I found opportunities to expand my knowledge and broaden my education.

If trust is earned, it can also be unearned, in which case it isn't trust. Trust must be learned, not earned. Earned trust can be a trap. We let go of a lot of self-awareness when we simply trust. We can miss the early warning signals, much like I did with Poco. Life and horses have kept me humble because I realize nothing is a given. Circumstances, feelings, and perceptions are changing all the time. I have learned it's best to change with life, not rely on a dependency of trust. Ray said, "Confidence is being prepared for the unimaginable." I can't say what that meant to Ray, but what it meant to me is that I have to keep adapting to the changes as well as working on myself. This keeps my mind in the game and open to learning. And this illustrates once again that the learning process begins within us.

If trust is earned, it can also be unearned, in which case it isn't trust. Trust must be learned, not earned.

Re-Minding

My first step may have been the hardest. It involved unlearning everything I thought I knew about trust and confidence. The early stage of re-minding myself of my own strengths and convictions involved releasing long-held paradigms of defense. The first act of learning trust was to trust myself. This meant letting go of the safety ropes that I believed held my security. These ropes were composed of my opinions and assumptions.

Truthfully, I found that these opinions of myself and others hung me on a shaky limb of oppression. I had to let go of the (perceived) need to control people, places, and things and trust what was in my heart. The only thing I know is my own truth. And even that can be blocked by an outward projection of what I *think* might "save" me. I realized through trial and error that the deeply unconscious need for security was actually a practice in fear, not a practice of trust. Trust was needed only when fear was present. I realized that if I kept working from a level of fear, trust would be forever elusive. As I came to understand this, I saw it as an awakening of sorts. My lifelong dependency on trust was completely unnecessary and actually held me back from feeling at ease.

Being enslaved by my dependency on trust for confidence was far more dangerous than opening my mind to my own internal consent. I first had to learn how to develop trust within myself while lacking confidence. This was a tricky first step in my process of unlearning fear and redeveloping my own confidence. I reminded myself of my choices and utilized the power of observation. I called this process re-minding because I was not pulling from something new. I was simply empowering what had been hidden and forgotten.

We all have an inherent trust within us. We have simply forgotten the early, embryotic stage of life when we trusted in all that is. This trust has never left us, though we learned to cover it up. We learned and acquired fear. This is a simplistic way of stating a complex aspect of the mind. Re-minding is returning to our natural state of well-being. It is a conscious decision to see things differently. And most especially, to let go of the thought process that insists well-being exists somewhere outside of us.

After I was bucked off, I reached much deeper into my relationship with Poco, though not a lot broader. It was an in-depth study within a narrow margin. I stayed within the limitations of my lowered self-confidence. While honoring my process of healing (both physically and mentally), I explored the degrees between zero and one intricately. I wanted to know all about Poco, and our relationship deepened intensely. I had skipped over the most essential, elemental aspect of the connection with this horse. I had taken him for granted. I had focused on *how* he was, not *who* he was. I had missed seeing deep into his heart. I was unaware of how he perceived the world. I hadn't been listening on a personal level. I had been focused on an outcome. After realizing all this, we could expand on these things as if we were beginning a brand-new relationship—because, indeed, we were.

There comes a time when, having gained some experience and regained equilibrium, we have to continue to move forward. There is a pivotal point that can either feed successful learning or feed the fear. Months after having hit the dirt, I had reached that point in the process. It was time to move ahead.

I took a bit of a hiatus from riding while I was starting over with Poco. Finally I saddled Far Go, my older, wiser horse. Far Go and I have seen a lot of life together, and I was longing for a ride where sheer enjoyment was the main objective. Far Go has never been a passive horse; he's full of life and full of spirit. At this point I had been focusing all my energy to restart Poco. So I had laid Far Go off for a couple of months. I had never had this long of a break from Far Go since I'd had him; he was typically my go-to horse. Before heading out for a jaunt up the road, I thought I had better check him out in the arena to be sure he was mentally ready. I rode for just a few moments before I said, "Come on, buddy, let's get out of here."

I noticed immediately how both of us were feeling the same way. It was long overdue, and as we headed up the drive, it felt right. Yet somewhere deep within myself, I noticed the lingering residue of fear from getting hurt when I fell off Poco. As we rounded the top of our drive and headed down the gravel road, I remembered the saying, "If you knew who walked beside you, you would never feel fear again." Only I quickly changed this to say, "If you knew who rode beside you, you would never feel fear again." At that moment I pictured clearly Ray and Tom on their horses, riding on either side of me. They were grinning those unmistakable grins. What joy I felt! It was like an instant internal release from fear. This experience revealed to me how quickly my thoughts could shift my feelings. I had used the vision of Ray and Tom many times in the arena to "raise the bar" and remind myself to listen or to "use a little less." I have visualized the two of them sitting in the chairs on the platform at the end of the arena. I ride as if they are watching me. But this was the first time I'd utilized this outside the arena.

There was something so comforting and balancing in sensing my great teachers there with me on horseback—like two bookends, holding me in their wisdom and offering support. Just after that I sighed and grinned. And then a small pygmy goat stepped out of the tall grass behind a fence along the road. The goat startled Far Go. For a horse, animals popping out of the grass ignite the natural instinct for flight; after all, that's where lions wander. I was able to support Far Go through his reaction. Well, that is, Tom, Ray, and I. Of course I am not using this as a literal statement, but that "sense" I felt a moment earlier was still resonating in my heart. I really think we underestimate ourselves too. We have a vast array of resources to pull from. We limit ourselves if we rely on only our thoughts. Far Go settled quickly, and we continued down the road. Neither one of us made more out of it than it was.

The thing about fear is that it feeds on reaction. If fear can get a stronghold, it can take off like a wildfire in a windstorm. There are countless degrees between surprise and fear. Far Go and I just went on by the goat and continued on our path. Soon a few neighboring horses came up to the fence and ran alongside us. My horse was much more interested in where we were going than socializing with those horses. This confirmed to me that Far Go had gained some additional confidence. He wasn't trading me in for those of his own kind. The unity felt good to both of us. As we turned the corner into a vineyard, there was a perfect path of soft, smooth dirt. I had a soft feel of the reins, and Far Go picked up a beautiful, balanced canter—one that I would be proud for the pope to ride.

I will never forget this day, with Tom and Ray riding along beside me. Now I have yet another gift from these great horsemen. I felt as if I increased my confidence as I sensed Ray and Tom's presence. I saw a lot of this at Ray Hunt clinics. Some people wouldn't believe they could succeed, but they believed in Ray. "Ray can." And if Ray could, and he asked them to try, they would try, and then they would find a success. It would be their own success, but it was as if they could dovetail off Ray's assurance.

Horses rely on others for confidence too. It is not unusual for them to look to the leader for support, whether that is another horse or a human. Horses have their doubts, but when we believe in their abilities, they will try. Overcoming fear is natural. The fear response is meant as a temporary effect, not a permanent way of life. If the alarm is never ending, it loses its effectiveness. The real benefit to gaining confidence is that it feels good! Horses want peace just as humans do. Living in fear is not living naturally—it's stressful on the mind and the body. Ray encouraged us to believe in our horse. To offer confidence is to gain it.

As we ride through our life, there are countless first-time experiences. There are unknowns in every day. Sometimes they are frightening. Learned trust is essential to enjoy and embrace our experience of life. When I was a child, my mother would say, "I don't know how people get through life if they don't believe in God." God can. This knowing helped my mother raise four children on her own, even though she was an orphan, adopted as an only child. She had no way of drawing from any past experience, yet she found trust in herself through her faith in God.

Overcoming fear is natural. The fear response is meant as a temporary effect, not a permanent way of life.

We can find trust in our own inner voice. This voice is real for us. Learning trust is learning to listen to God within. This need not be a controversial message. The God within can be simply your deepest heart. Keep in mind that the heart—or love, as I like to call it—has no opposite. The learned habit of fear and judgment is always conflicting with something. We can use these conflicts as tools to re-mind ourselves to listen more closely. We can be observant and seek to understand on a deeper level what our life situation is offering us. Fear becomes dysfunctional only when we identify with it as our reality. This is the empowering quality I found in my experience with Poco. Poco taught me to listen, and he taught me in the only way I knew at the time, through conflict.

I began to see signals of conflict in my horse and in my life as a simplistic alarm system. They are there to notify me that I have returned to my habit of fear. Now I use this alarm to bring me back home to my own inner trust.

I realized I can ask for help in the re-minding process. Just as Ray and Tom were right there with me the moment I was willing to see them, so is my own inner guidance. That inner light is infinite and radiating. It cannot be undone, outdone, incomplete, ineffective, outdistanced, or unavailable. The only way that I can possibly miss this elemental attribute of who I am is if I look away from it.

The birthright of my own free will is also infinite and unconditional. This is why perfect practice is so important to me. Mindful practice reminds me that I have a choice. I can choose where I find my confidence. I can ask myself, *Is it true or counterfeit? Do I own it, or is it rented?* True confidence is the by-product of learned trust. Disappointment, betrayal, and heartbreak come from someone else's opinion. This is a sure sign that dependency has been misinterpreted as trust.

It is easy to unconsciously become habituated in thinking that something has to happen outside of me to feel at peace. We can easily forget that all the sensations that accompany trust and confidence exist inside us. Consciously I realized that trust is an inner feeling, not a conditional response. Everyone can have trust when it comes from *within*. It is only scarce when it is something we are trying for. Far Go, Ray, and Tom helped me re-mind myself of my inner trust so I could more effectively connect with Poco and all life.

Building a Practice

The most meaningful work I do in life or with horses is that of the heart. I felt inspired by the whole concept of horsemanship when I learned from Ray that everything I do with my horse has a purpose and a meaning. My actions have a very real effect, and I need to be keenly aware of them. Horsemanship made me cognizant of the connection between my intentions and my actions. The horse became my mirror. With horses and in life, it's easy to become task oriented. All too often we forget about meaning and purpose. When we are focused on an outcome, we can end up checking our heart (and our consciousness) at the gate. When we go to work, clean the house, do the shopping, pay bills, travel, or carry out any of the countless daily experiences of life, we forget. The task is not what matters in the big picture. What matters is the awareness of the amount of time we spend in the "forgetting practice." The word *for-get* illustrates that we are living in misbelief, that we are seeking something we already have. I found that like horses, we, too, learn what we live. If I want to find the inner guidance of trust, confidence, and peace, I must practice living from the source of these attributes, and that source is within me.

My teacher Joe Wolter was coming to do a private clinic at my place. I was primed to learn new ways of helping Poco succeed and find true and lasting confidence for us both. Joe is a great man and a wonderful teacher in his own right. He also spent a lot of time with both Ray and Tom, and I respect him as a prime example of their legacy. It was the morning of the clinic, and my husband left to pick up Joe from his bed-and-breakfast lodging. I was hurrying around to have everything ready. It is always so exciting to get to spend time with Joe. I love sharing this experience with friends and my husband. We all get to learn so much about ourselves and our horses.

As I was saddling the horses, I saw Joe walking down the path. I felt like a schoolgirl who was late for class. School was never my thing, and it seems I have had a lifetime of practicing nerves around it. Clinics often rekindle these ancient unconscious traits. I had finished saddling Poco and was saddling Far Go when Joe walked up and said, "Good morning." He then took a step back, looked at Poco, and asked "Mary, who is that buckskin horse?" I said, "That's Poco, the one I told you about." When Joe and I had visited the night before, I had told him about Poco bucking in the arena earlier that year. As Joe looked at Poco standing there tied, he said, "He doesn't look good." I looked over and saw Poco standing perfectly still, not even blinking. And that was the point. He wasn't even blinking. He was frozen. Immediately I saw what Joe was seeing. I had overlooked the whole purpose of this day because I was just trying to get him saddled. I took for granted the most important step of the process, the first one. My habit of saddling without being aware of how Poco felt showed up first thing. My lesson with Joe started right then and there. I had to back up and begin again. To develop a new practice, I couldn't settle for doing what I had always done. I unsaddled and started over, being vigilant of every step.

When I hear "I am just trying to get it done," it sends a red flag flying for me. This striving mind is in a hurry. It is projecting the results of the task into some far-off future, not focusing on the purpose. The results take care of themselves when we stay conscious of the purpose. The whole reason I'd asked Joe to get on an airplane and fly out here to visit was so I could learn to "get with" my horse. The first thing I did was lose my focus with Poco; I just got him saddled so we could start the day. Heck, the day started the moment I haltered him. Thank goodness horses have the forgiveness of saints in their hearts. And I had a do-over! That clinic, like all the clinics in my life, taught me a lot about myself. The source of my horsemanship is my heart. It must start within me. Just like trust and confidence, meaning and purpose need clarity from the source.

Counterfeit Confidence

It is important to recognize that the derivative of trust is confidence. If I allow myself to practice feeling afraid, I will be really good at fear. But when I slow down, check in, and work from my own observations, I find success and learn to trust my own judgment. This builds true confidence. It's the same way with horses. If they do something from willingness, they retain confidence. If they are forced to do something, they can retain the resistance to it. When we learn that we are empowered with the ability to succeed in a fearful situation, it is a practice in true and lasting confidence. When we depend on something outside of us for trust, it's temporary and subject to change; this is a practice in fear. Therefore, confidence can be either real or counterfeit based on where we draw it from. It's like drinking from a mountain stream. My mustang Concho knew the difference between stagnant and running water. I remember years ago riding him into a river to drink. There was a log that had sectioned off some water that looked pretty easy to get to. But when I rode him into it, he stepped over the log to get to the moving water. As a wild horse, he knew things that my domestic horses didn't know. Concho was keenly aware of his environment and had excellent survival skills. Like the water in the stream, the difference in true or counterfeit confidence is the clarity of the source. It is the awareness of the source of our trust that offers the reward of peace.

Trusting that an outside source "gives" us confidence can set us up for vulnerability. This is another "fine, cavernous line" to cross. Of course we must trust in others. We trust that other cars on the road are not going to crash into us, or we trust the bank to hold our savings. Trust is extremely important in day-to-day life. When learning to trust from our deepest attention, we also learn that it is not so much that we trust others as that we trust our decision to trust.

After I got hurt falling off Poco and lost a lot of confidence, I realized I was looking to the outcomes to trust my horse. I thought if I stayed safe, I could trust him. This was a very conditional way of living. I saw very clearly in that experience that I could easily wind up a victim of circumstance. Instead I owned what happened, and that helped me take ownership for our future.

It is important to recognize that the derivative of trust is confidence. If I allow myself to practice feeling afraid, I will be really good at fear.

I made a deal with myself and my horse that I would not get on if he showed any signs of bucking. This was my "100 percent rule." I was definitely shaken, and I needed some good experience to regain my confidence. I opted to do only what felt right for me. All bets were off. I made a conscious decision to work from a success to a success. There may have been hundreds of other opinions about getting back on and riding, but the only opinion that mattered was mine. I built my inner trust from listening to my inner voice.

Some days I would come out of the house and be excited to go work with Poco because I saw the progress. We had several good sessions, and I felt that we were really developing an understanding based on what was real for both of us. Our level of trust was on the upswing. I would think, *Maybe today I get to ride.* But then he would jump or flinch or kick out, and I held to my 100 percent rule. I recognized that I felt a sense of disappointment. I allowed that feeling to be there, but that feeling did not make the decisions! I would then begin again and find the beauty in the moment, right there where we were. I became more open and aware of how I could help us both build confidence.

There are certain exercises that I had learned twenty-five years ago that all of a sudden had so much more meaning and purpose. I said out loud, "Oh wow, that's what that is all about!" It was as if I had cleared some dense fog that was between my horse and me. The fog was simple counterfeit confidence. I thought I knew what I needed to know to be a sensitive partner with my horse. As it turned out, all that I had learned was just a starter course. It was both humbling and exhilarating. I then set out to revisit all the areas that I had taken for granted. I began listening to Ray's words in my mind with a brand-new perspective.

The experience of building a foundation of true trust reminded me of the most important practice of all: listening to my own inner voice. From that place of personal understanding, I can also honor what my horse is feeling. Once I realized the benefits of learning trust and true confidence with Poco, it carried over into the rest of my life. I began to experience much greater success. I was willing to take more risks, have more fun, love deeper, and even see a vast array of beauty in places I never even knew existed. I started to look at the next bend in the road with excitement and enthusiasm. Even the challenges were less overwhelming because I trusted myself to stay present within my compassionate heart.

Beyond Trust: Freedom

The deeper understanding that I was working with a mind when riding my horse was probably the most valuable thing I could have learned in my horsemanship. It seems so obvious, but it is quite often overlooked. We are not riding machines. Horses can feel, sense, differentiate, learn, understand, mature, and develop. They can also do the opposite; they can zone out or lose their mind. People do this too. When life becomes unfulfilling or uninspiring, horses and people can become unconscious. It is very easy to lose sight of our purpose and meaning and return to the habit of fear. Fear takes us far away from our inner balance and well-being. Being mindful was my tether to truth, the elixir from illusion. I realized real trust was not found in a constantly changing world. Deeply understanding the benefits of working with the mind became a vital part of realizing success.

I am most effective when I do not resist. This happens in my life when I am in the natural flow of my "accepting mind." The accepting mind does not mean settling for what I don't want. It simply means accepting what actually is happening in this moment and being responsible for my decisions about it. My best decisions come from my open and conscious mind. Not when I am defensive and reactive. This positive practice rescued me from the dangling, shaky limb of dependency on others. I also learned I could respond to life authentically.

If a horse tells me through his actions or reactions that he is tight or braced, or I see that he wants to flee or buck, I do not have to make a judgment about right or wrong but simply make a decision about what is best for us as a whole. I know I cannot help him feel better if I am insecure or injured. The last thing I would want to do is overlook the brace and climb on. Yet this is often how I would deal with life experiences. I would sense that things weren't quite right in my life, and yet I would continue to push right through them. I would just try to get to the other side where I felt good again. I missed so much of what I needed to learn by just getting through things rather than learning from them. When I lived my life through the habit of survival, I often felt betrayed or abandoned. Then, as the cycle dictated, I would lose trust. In all reality, the first one who abandoned me was me. When we don't understand real trust, we tend to think things should be different than they are. That thought only adds resistance to our life. Real change comes from seeing things as they are and then deciding accordingly.

From the accepting mind, I learned nonresistance. And from nonresistance comes nonduality. When my mind can learn nonduality as a philosophy, I am free. To me, this is the most valuable of all lessons, but first I must learn to live free from my dependency on trust. Freedom is my ultimate reward. I do not make light of this. I emphasize that it is the ultimate goal.

While on my way toward real freedom, I have lots of practice mindfully opening my heart, my perceptions, and my fears. I can gain a wider, deeper perspective. The journey to freedom requires me to let go of fear as my guide. I need not let go of discernment to let go of fear. I have found that fear is limiting; it closes my mind. Discernment united my instinct of survival with my desire for peace. Together they enhance my life through developing a practice of acceptance.

I remember the early days when I first saw Ray Hunt. There were a lot of people who would say, "I don't have time to spend on that nonsense." I always thought, *You don't have time not to.* There seems to be a tendency for people to see change as time consuming. With this mind-set it is easy to get stuck focusing on the investment for change rather than the benefits of it. I see that this narrow-mindedness is most common when we feel the current practice is adequate. I realized that a big block to the willingness for something new comes when we live from comfortable mediocrity. Trusting that things won't change is a flawed system. Eventually everything changes. It can sometimes cause a lot of grief to just wait until things go wrong to change them up. Being proactive is being effective. We grow as we go.

Change is challenging even when it is absolutely the best option. An example of this in my life is when I clean the barn. I use my right side as my predominant side. My wrist and shoulder have worn out from years of this repeated motion. As the pain got worse, I began to realize that I had a perfectly good left side that I could use. I started to use my left hand and was thrilled that I was pain-free. With that said, within moments, without even realizing it, I was back to using my right side. Even though my habit caused a lot of pain, I would still mindlessly default to it. So it is in life. "Change is good" must be our creed to overcome centuries of acquired fear. The key to positive change begins with a positive mind.

I found a new world when I learned trust and practiced confidence. I evolved past my acquired belief that trust is earned, that it must come from outside circumstances. I saw my own response-ability to the outcomes in my life. I gained confidence through my own power of discernment, as well as asking for help when I needed support. I began to recognize and accept that I was in the process of learning to trust myself and wanted to let go of my reliance on outside circumstances to create my security.

I found a new world when I learned trust and practiced confidence. I evolved past my acquired belief that trust is earned, that it must come from outside circumstances.

I also realized there is a paradox in the idea that control leads to peace. Unveiling this enigma released my mind and opened my options, adding a much greater perspective. I developed my own inner trust, which in turn offered real and lasting confidence.

This in-depth study spans the all-inclusive mind; the intellect, emotions, and intentions all play a role in true confidence. Perfect practice can offer a release from the dependency on trust itself, ultimately offering a perspective of nonduality. Nonduality is freedom from unconscious thoughts, and therein lies the treasure of perfect practice.

CHAPTER NINE

Worthiness

Honesty is what I love in horses. Honesty in horses helps me find the same in myself. I often use my love for the horse as a guide to loving everything, especially people. You might say horses teach me what the world at large hasn't.

I know I'm not alone when I say that through much of my life I lacked a sense of worthiness. This unworthiness tainted most everything I did. I felt like I didn't fit in anywhere, and this affected my life experiences and promoted a habit of fear. I felt falsely judged when I was young, and even now, if I am not fully conscious, that same fear will appear in current situations and initiate a feeling of separation. This well-practiced sense of unworthiness prevented my mind and heart from opening completely.

As I got older, I realized how my early interpretations of other people's opinions were negatively affecting my life. I finally realized that I was blindly following opinions that were not at all true. As I began to recognize this, I started to grow into my self-worth. This really inspired me. In fact, without worthiness this book couldn't have been written. Worthiness is required for authentic expression and for fulfillment in my life. I had to be willing to be vulnerable and trust in my deepest calling. I had to be an open vessel to share and receive fully. Judgment, defense, perception, and false truth closed me off from others and shamed me out of believing in myself. This book, in a sense, is my coming-of-age party.

When I bought my first horse, I was so inspired that I got lost in the passion of it all. I began creating higher and higher expectations for myself and my horse. I lost sight of the present moment and began looking to the future for my rewards. I think this is very common when it comes to feeling passionate about something. The passion has a momentum all its own. We start living our life at an accelerated speed. This was when I started heading south, from love to expectations. There was a definitive line that I was crossing unconsciously. I am forever grateful for the wisdom of Tom Dorrance through the teachings of Ray Hunt. Being exposed to their wisdom was the tether to my own truth.

I loved hearing Ray share what he learned from Tom. A lot of times when talking about Tom, he would simply say, "My friend speaks of it as…" Well, we all knew what friend Ray was referring to. I knew because there would be this certain sparkle in Ray's eye. It seemed to come from deep within him. There was no doubt of the respect and admiration that Ray felt for his friend. Ray recognized something very different in how horses responded to Tom. This subtle difference was something I think Ray wanted to find in himself. What Tom did with the horse was so subtle that he couldn't put a finger on it. Tom would just show up and horses improved. At first it seemed undetectable, but Ray knew there was something there. There was a deep connection and understanding between the horse and Tom. Ray could see it, and he knew that he wanted to develop that quality in himself. Ray was dedicated to improving himself for the sake of the horse. He did this for the rest of his life. Ray said, "I'm just seeing pieces of it. But I'll never leave that part out, never—ever!"

Ray explained that this spirit or this piece was lying dormant in the horse, just waiting for the opportunity to be expressed. I was intrigued. I could listen to Ray talk all day. His stories of Tom are still alive in my mind. Ray told about how Tom could fix things up (for the horse) then wait for the change in the horse to show itself. In other words, Tom knew how to open the door for the horse to express himself authentically so that it was a mind in relationship with another mind. It wasn't just whip and spur and "get 'er done." This is where Tom's beauty with the horse was so apparent to me. It was through seeing the life in the horse, the true spirit, the individual. It was in showing respect, compassion, and admiration. All these things and so much more played a role in opening the channel for true communication with the horse—just as it does in all relationships. What Tom was capable of naturally, most of us had never even seen. Although on some level, I feel, it must be within us all. But it's buried behind our thoughts and interpretations. Sometimes the messages almost felt cryptic. I would have to let them soak for months or even years to understand a fraction of the lessons. I wonder if that's how it was for Ray in the beginning when Tom first shared these things with him.

The stories Ray told became legends. They have been told so many times that, like any good tale, the message is what's important. The details of any story can easily get lost in translation. One such story is of a conversation between Tom and Ray. Tom asked Ray to wait. And Ray questioned how long do we wait, and for what are we waiting? The story goes that Tom once waited seven years. Ray shared that there was no way to *make* this nuance we are waiting for happen—you must allow it to happen. I have pondered over this story for decades. All I could infer is that what I was waiting for was the horse's mind, willingness of heart, and authentic spirit to show itself in our relationship. I sensed that is why Ray couldn't identify what "it" was. It is indeed unexplainable. The awareness of this true spirit and the respect for that essence are what I learned to wait for. Ray taught this to me through my horsemanship, but like all the lessons I received, it wasn't exclusive to horses. I also learned it for my life.

I think people can live their whole lives and not even realize what is missing. It seems many are able to sense an emptiness or a void in themselves but not identify it. This can cause them to try to fill it in with approval or accomplishment, or mask it with a substance or find resentment and anger for the world. We can search and search outside ourselves for "enough" to fill the void. But if we are not looking inward, we can't quite identify the source of that hollow space within. The pain of "something is missing" leads us to find that spark within. That spark is in every sentient being, in every expression of life. That spark is patient. It waits for our recognition, sometimes lying dormant for countless years, until the barriers of fear are released and the life spark can be revealed in all its grace and majesty. When we let down the assumptions of our acquired expectations and allow our true spirit to shine through, we begin to see the ultimate worth of life itself.

I think people can live their whole lives and not even realize what is missing. It seems many are able to sense an emptiness or a void in themselves but not identify it.

Ray was masterful at setting things up and allowing the change to happen with the horse. To me this embodies all the elements of trust, faith, confidence, and worthiness—I needed to recognize all of this in myself in order to have a fulfilling life and authentic relationships. Ray did convey that a hurdle to doing this effectively is that you have to fix it so it *can* work. If you want a horse to reach for you, accept you, and feel safe with you, you can't force him into it. And if you start to get too pushy, he'll just take off. It's just too much pressure. But if you stand too far off and he needn't even acknowledge your existence, it isn't going to happen either. There is a dance, an exchange of ideas, that takes place. It is not a stagnant, flat energy. It moves and develops; it is vibrant and pulsating. And though the idea is unspoken, it is in no way restrained. This is a dance that we all experience within every interaction. But our expectations and our preconceptions dull the senses; they blind us to the true nature of "relationship." Our relationships are where the true worth of our life can be found. Even if (and perhaps especially when) that relationship is the one between our acquired identity and our own true spirit. This is where the real magic can appear in life and from which all true relationships spawn.

In hindsight, I can see how my relationships have matured as my understanding of the horse has progressed. My love for horses opened my heart, introducing me to my own sense of worthiness. It has taken many years, several horses, and countless human relationships (both failed and successful) to begin to scale the jagged border between my true self-worth and perceived unworthiness. Life continues to hand me experiences to cultivate the ground on which I stand. How I traverse the terrain of my life dictates my allegiance or my surrender. I grow through nurturing the relationship of self and spirit, or die in resistance. The outcomes lay like tombstones in my past. They are all markers of effective or ineffective relating. But it all comes down to my relationship with life.

The details vary greatly, but the emotional responses don't. Horses come in varying details as well. Some are highly demonstrative and others passive and shy. How we relate to them can seem very different, though the end result will be either unification or separation. So it is with all relationships, big or small.

The Gift

The culmination of all my life processes came to a peak experience when I met the love of my life, my husband, Magnus. The moment I saw him, I knew the final exam was near. This was the test of my resolve, beliefs, and of my commitment for my heart to lead the way. It was a pop quiz in worthiness that has been followed by an advanced education in relationships. This time in my life was unnerving and completely stripped me of my historical defenses. I somehow knew the value of the experience before I knew what the experience would be. Much in the same way that Ray knew Tom had something of great value, though he could scarcely identify it in words—he knew it! Ray took the steps that Tom asked him to take. He had faith in this spot in his heart that he had never met before. If Ray hadn't listened to his heart, the world of horses would be a very different place today.

Listening to wordless messages may be what some label a calling. You just know without overthinking it. You trust without knowing what it is you are trusting in. It was poetic timing that I met my husband while working with a horse and my soon-to-be stepson.

It was Father's Day, and Magnus had brought his son for a riding lesson. I don't consider myself a riding instructor; I never have. But in this unique time of my life, I had been asked to teach some kids. A friend I had helped with a horse that was kicking and bucking also had a young daughter in a private school. When I was at her place working with the horse, I also shared what I was doing with the little girl. Children are brilliant at sensing the reverence for life that I was offering to this horse. This little girl loved being with the horse in this way. Soon her mother told other mothers, and my phone was ringing off the hook.

I told the first lady who called, "I am sorry, I don't work with children, and frankly I don't teach riding. I help people get along with their horses." This woman would not take no for an answer. I somehow felt that it was important not to insist on closing doors that seemed to be forced open. Next thing I knew, there were eighteen children on a field trip in my arena, one of whom would eventually become my stepson. Allowing these kids to come into my life and letting go of my resistance to the idea offered me the ultimate gift of my lifetime.

At fifty years old, I had come to a place of peace in my life. I'd made a pact with myself not to settle for less than a love that cannot be defined by action, status, wealth, or prestige. This was not avoidance; it was indeed acceptance. I had settled countless times for relationships that were a blueprint from someone else's design. These relationships were not of my soul but of my acquired identity. One ex-partner had a saying that fit this turnstile to a tee: "Lookin' good, goin' nowhere."

I knew of the spark that burned in my heart, yet I also knew it had a life of its own to live. I knew it was not something I could force or make happen. Much like "fix it up and wait." I was content to wait, even if it meant into the great beyond. I suppose if someone asked me how long I waited for this light to have its life, I could say, "I waited fifty years once." Recognizing this light reflecting back from Magnus's eyes was only the beginning.

Magnus stepped out of his pearl-black Jeep Wrangler and right into my heart. It's funny how I tried to shut that door just like I had tried to shut the door to the kids. By the time I met Magnus, I had already been working with his son for quite some time. I felt a kinship with this boy, his brother, and their mother. I liked this young family of three, and it seemed they liked me. I knew that they lived apart from their father, and I had not yet met him. As Magnus and his son walked into the barn, I took the child's hand and headed to the arena. I couldn't look back for fear that my initial heartfelt reaction was still there. I was happy in my life. I finally felt at peace. I couldn't imagine muddying up the water.

After the lesson, I led the horse into the pasture and said out loud, "What just happened?" I was questioning this energy I felt rising from a deeply hallowed place in my soul. Then I received an email from Magnus telling me how impressed he was that I focused all my attention on his son. I didn't let on that that was because I was afraid to look through that door. After several email correspondences, Magnus finally asked me out for dinner. I was so independent at the time that I couldn't imagine Magnus was asking me on a date. I thought he was just interested in being friends. I agreed and suggested that we meet for tea.

The following Sunday evening we met on the lawn at a local coffee shop. We talked well into the night, and as the sun was setting, he said he would like to see me again. Even then I wasn't completely sure if this was leading to something more romantic. I suggested that since I was his son's riding instructor, I felt it important to ask his ex-wife for her approval. I will never forget what she said that day I asked. She said she had just been telling her partner, "I wish that Magnus would find someone we could all love." And then she gave me her blessing. My life began a brand-new incarnation in that moment. Little did I know of all that was to come. I was scared, excited, love drunk, confused, and blindsided by it all. But within the first week, I knew I was all in. Some things you just have to allow your heart to choose.

My mind had already taken me down some rough roads. This time, I decided to follow my heart.

The Stock Tank Miracle

As Magnus and I moved with passion through the early stages of our relationship, we were faced with a meteor shower of emotions. Bombarded with everything from bliss to bizarre, our worlds were upside down. That is just what this kind of intensity offers. There is a saying with horses: "Everything happens in the transition." Often it goes north or south, good or bad, while transitioning from one thing to another or from one level of understanding to the next. Such is life. Change instigates growth, and at times growth can involve a lot of pain. I was in for big changes in my life, initiating intense transitions. I was going to have to test my resolve. This certainly was not a time to be hurrying through things or relying on my thoughts and past fears. I was going to need to pull from that deeper self I had come to love. I realized that was not going to be easy. But I had done my personal work, and I felt I was ready. This was the ultimate test of my sense of worthiness for such a love. There was now a dynamic energy. It was no longer a solitary study. All my years of learning from the horses, learning to trust my senses over my intellect and to feel instead of judge, were about to pay off in stardust, but not before the final exam.

The three-year period in my life before I met Magnus was a very solitary experience. I made my living from home, and I didn't date or do much socializing outside the canyon where I lived. I felt content and sheltered within the canyon walls. I spent my free time genuinely looking deeply into who I had become. I suppose you could say I was entering a midlife transition. My focus was on my desire for an effective and peaceful shift. I wanted to be very clear as to how I created the second half of my life. I often say, "That God, what a kidder." I really had no idea what was around the next bend. But I did know one thing for certain: I was never going to leave my worthiness behind again.

Worthiness had not been a part of my doctrine up to this point. In fact, most of my tenacious qualities came from insecurity, not confidence. I was determined, all right! But this determination was bred from a lack of trust in people, and after many devoted applications of this sort of thinking, I elected to learn how to really love and respect myself.

Worthiness had not been a part of my doctrine up to this point. In fact, most of my tenacious qualities came from insecurity, not confidence.

I remember clearly when this inner lamp was lit. It was at the end of my last relationship, before my reprieve. My ex-partner had already moved out, yet he was still hovering over me, telling me how flawed I was. One day the winds of time stood still, the clouds broke apart, and I finally looked him square in the eye and said, "Your negative opinion of me is inaccurate." He kept on ranting, yet what I had said was not for him at all. He most likely never even heard it. But I meant it. I owned it, and for the first time in my entire life, I believed it!

It all happened in the transition. At this crossroads in my life, I made a solemn vow to Mary. I started listening on a much deeper level to all my heart and soul messages. It seemed they had been wrapped neatly in tight little packages and stored behind my tendency to please others. These gifts had been safely locked away until such time as I was ready to receive them. Finding this part of me was like opening an old hope chest in my heart. This was when I freed myself from the "shame that binds."

I set out to let go of narrow-minded opinions, and I began with my own. I changed how I saw myself. I spent a great deal of time in the canyon, just learning to listen. I was curious. What was this light that I had always sensed in my heart but never clearly understood? I knew I was moving toward something, and I knew that "something" was good. This inner warmth felt a lot like what I imagined love to be. The important difference was that it was a love that lived inside of me, not in an outside source. One clue that led me to understand it as love was that I knew it was meant to be shared. I had no specific ideas as to how or when or who, and the funny thing was, none of that really mattered. I was inspired to include it in everything I did—my work with horses, my work with people, and my creations in the canyon. I wrote, I read, and I explored with an open mind and an open heart. I fed the baby, and the baby was worthiness.

The world at large demands performance. We learn how to perform early in our lives. We have to make the grade to advance in school. We have to win out over others to get a job. We have to be "good enough" for someone to fall in love with us. We identify with being a good person, a good daughter, and so on. We learn performance, but performance can decay worthiness. Like pounding surf eroding solid rock, my inherent completeness diminished over time in my mind but…only in my mind. After years of destruction, I scanned the rubble of my failed relationships, missed opportunities, and countless regrets to find a voice coming from below the dust. Wait! There's life down there. I started to dig through the broken pieces and uncover my truth once again—untarnished and perfectly intact. This was the awakening of my own heart. When I shared this experience with another, I realized my ultimate truth. All my relationships were mirrors, and all offered me exactly (and only) what I was willing to see. As I emerged from the rubble and found my love in the eyes of another, I accepted my own divine worth.

Bonding takes loving care. Whether it is with a horse or a human, it is a process, and within the process is pain. Ancient, unrealized, and misunderstood, this pain is often reflected in blame, fear, resistance, and defense. This is the nature of seeing the world as hostile. This is what I came to understand. My perception of the world was really the instigator of my hostility.

As I emerged from the rubble and found my love in the eyes of another, I accepted my own divine worth.

Having just emerged from his own personal rubble, Magnus was not yet ready to fully open his heart. The years prior to meeting him had offered me the great opportunity of time and space to nourish my flickering spark within. This I had done in the shelter of my solitude. Magnus had not yet had his time. He still felt the hollowness and the pain of a hostile world. I wanted to be a soft place to fall and offer the space he needed. I came to know love, but not because I loved him or felt that he loved me, but by having the experiences that led me out of fear. I had choices this time, but they were not the choices of my past. They were not dualistic, as in "stay or go." The choice I learned to make was between fear and love.

In my time of need, I utilized the life lessons I learned in horsemanship. I knew to give the process the necessary time it needed to develop. I also recognized that I had to set things up to succeed. This meant staying focused on what I held as truth.

I somehow knew what truth felt like, though I had never recognized it before. My mind, my fear, and my doubts were rattling at the edge of my devotion. I held true, and then I would weaken to doubt and wonder, after so many failed relationships, *Is love real?* One question I asked myself over and over during this time was, *Is love enough?*

I would not deny the love I knew to be real, though I did need some guidance. I feared if Magnus could not open to the love I was offering, what then? I called on my trusted counselor for help. I left him a phone message saying, "Love is real." But by the time I made it to my appointment, I said, "Love is real, but is it enough?" My counselor, who had known me for more than a decade, said, "Enough for what?" As is with all great teachers, they know they can't give you your answer. Instead they ask great questions. I returned home to my fears and doubts but felt strengthened by my inquiry.

In life sometimes things get worse before they get better, and that they did. Magnus was in his rally of resistance, and we were scheduled to leave the next day for a weeklong trip to the Olympic Peninsula and Canada. I was taking two horses to a clinic, and we were taking a side trip to Victoria, British Columbia. Leaving for a week involved focus and attention to detail, planning for the house sitter and caring for the animals we were leaving behind.

Leaving home is a vulnerable state for me, and it was intensely compounded by Magnus's collapse into his fear. This was a transition in his life, the magnitude of which could be felt but not identified. It was a tumultuous time, and emotions were surfacing and changing faster than we could begin to understand them. Within this surreal moment in time, it seemed I had a decision to make. I considered the duality within my fear. Should I stay, or should I go? There it was, that question that fear asks. The limiting forces of fearful thoughts offer only two choices. These two can seem like choosing between the lesser of two evils. Stay and suffer, or leave and sacrifice. I had to choose to either rise above or go down with the ship. I had to meet my fear head-on.

I walked out to the pasture to fill the stock tank with water. As I stood there in pain, in fear and in suffering, not knowing what the next moment (let alone the next day) would bring, I asked right out loud to God as I know him to be, "God, am I devaluing myself in this relationship?" My fear was that I had left my worthiness once again and that I was settling for something other than love. I had never shared this part of myself with another human being. I had no road map, no navigation skills, nothing but past fear to draw from. I rarely go to the highest court for an answer. This, too, was part of the learning process in recognizing my own worthiness.

No sooner had I said it, and as clear as the water pouring from the spigot filled the tank, the answer filled my soul. God said only this: "You asked to love...you love."

And I said, "You know—you've got a point."

It's So Simple, It's Difficult

That trip north was a necessary journey. The darkness before the dawn asks of us our surrender. Magnus would be faced with surrendering the pain that blocked his love, and I would surrender my opinion of what I thought love was. It was a perfect storm. We both took hard hits in the process.

Back at home the horse I had left behind had lacerated her eye, and I was dealing with the vet by phone. Taking an extended three-day holiday before the clinic meant I had to leave my other two horses in the care of the clinic hosts. They were strangers to me, but I had felt okay about it, based on the conversations

over the phone. It was only for a couple of extra nights while
we skipped over to Victoria.

The darkness before the dawn asks of us our surrender.

Once we arrived at the barn, the sense of welcome I'd felt
before shifted to a lot of fear. I was not dealing with the wife,
who seemed knowledgeable and kind, but with her husband.
Now all that we had agreed on over the phone had suddenly
changed. The couple had completely opposing game plans. For
instance, I had asked if I should bring hay. Often bringing hay
to other areas introduces weeds that are not native and can be
seen as invasive. The wife had said, "No, don't bring hay," yet
when I arrived, the husband was saying something very different.
The more I talked with him, the worse I was feeling. I was wary
of leaving my horses with strangers to begin with, and now it
seemed I had some real valid concerns. I started to question if
any of this was a good idea. I was now six hours from home and
heading to another country and leaving my horses with a terrible
feeling in my gut. It seemed with each turn the nightmare was
getting worse. I found myself backing into a very dark corner.

Trust and confidence were not what I was gaining at this
point. I felt the ground crumbling beneath my feet. We went
to Victoria in spite of my nervousness about it. The next three
days felt as false as our perceptions about love and worthiness.
I was terrified. But I never told Magnus. I felt as if I was with
a stranger, yet I went on pretending we were on some honey-
moon vacation. I watched while all that I valued crumbled. This
was the divine process that the darkness was offering. I had to
let it all go so I could see what was real. While we were there I

felt more and more worried about my horses being boarded at the clinic barn. After three days of failed attempts to reach the barn owners, I could hardly wait to return to my horses and the comfort of what I intrinsically loved.

The horse clinic began, and Magnus retreated to the hotel room. I went to the clinic alone and found that my lessons were only beginning. The whole experience began to seem surreal. This was my new horse Poco's first clinic back when I still believed he was gentle as a lamb. On the first day of the clinic, Poco bucked me off. And although I injured my ribs, I climbed back on and finished the class, then I returned Poco to his stall. I was still trying to stay strong and have a positive attitude. On the second day, Poco did a lot better in his morning class, and I thought perhaps we would all finally be able to enjoy ourselves and settle into a learning frame of mind. I was also relieved that the horse I had brought for the cattle class was my clinic veteran Far Go. That was until I realized that four days of being cooped up together in adjoining stalls in an unfamiliar environment had created a strong bond of security between Poco and Far Go.

The cattle class was in a different location on the ranch from where the horses were stalled. Far Go was intensely anxious about being separated from Poco. He was having trouble accepting the approaching herd of cattle and bawling calves that were being driven in from the field. They were coming right into the pen that we were standing by. I had ridden Far Go with cows before, but only a small bunch. And they were very passive. This looked as if it were a sea of a hundred or more cows running right toward him. His anxiety was escalating.

I had ridden Far Go earlier in the class, where we practiced cattle work with a string cow. A string cow is a remote-controlled plastic flag that moves back and forth along the fence.

I was never able to settle Far Go down, and truthfully I knew we were merely surviving. By the time they brought the cattle in, it was getting late. I had to leave to meet my family who was driving down from Seattle. I was so mentally exhausted that I could not think a clear thought. I decided to unsaddle and clean the stalls in preparation for the night. I was told it would be good for Far Go to stand tied near the cattle. They told me, "Let him grow up." Much against my gut feeling, I trusted this advice. The people there promised me they would look after him. At this point, I certainly felt it better to trust their judgment over my own. As I drove away, I saw my horse, my longtime friend and partner, standing there tied. I could see that Far Go looked exactly like I felt—lost, scared, and alone. This feeling was more than I could bear. For the first time on this entire trip, I finally just fell apart.

To this day, my one true regret from this experience was that I left Far Go tied up there to work it out. I would never do that again. Far Go and I were both so mentally and emotionally depleted by then that neither one of us could conceive of a learning frame of mind. There was no way we were prepared to just stand there and work it out. I felt I had no self-worth left. I had exhausted my capacity to endure another hit. No degree of training was worth that amount of fear. It all worked out, however. The folks who watched over him returned Far Go to his stall that evening. But after that day, I vowed to Far Go that I would never leave him in that way again…never ever.

The next morning I surrendered. I woke battered and bruised—mentally, physically, and emotionally. I said, "Enough! I want to go home." I was done, my horses were done, and Magnus was still in some faraway place. This was a first. I had never left in the middle of a clinic. To me, leaving would be quitting. And quitting would indeed validate my inflamed sense of unworthiness. That combined with sacrificing a large financial investment created a strong defense against listening to my heart. I couldn't just keep being strong. I had no more performance left in me. This was my dark night of the soul. This was when I let go of trying to be someone who I wasn't. I let go of trying to be a good student, a good girlfriend, or even a worthy individual. I was injured and raw, and that very pain is what taught me to let go of the world's opinions. This included my teachers and Magnus, all very influential people in my life. The dark night of the soul is what forced me to return to my deepest self and find my own sense of worthiness again.

I said to Magnus, "Pack up, we're going home." It turns out home was much larger than the canyon. Home was returning to my own self-worth. At a low point on the trip, I had called my cousin, a woman I love and respect. I wanted to talk over my frustrations about my relationship with Magnus. She said, "Honey, maybe you just have to let him go." I responded, "I will not. Magnus may leave me, but it will not be with my help." Even through the depths of my pain, I remembered the Stock Tank Miracle. And a miracle it was. I've heard it said a miracle is the shift from fear to love. I was on the edge between these two worlds and walking on fragmented glass. The Stock Tank Miracle taught me true and lasting love. The six-word message whispered into my soul that day described in undeniable detail how to love. It showed me what was false in my perceptions about love.

The Stock Tank Miracle showed me the one and only response to love is love. Everything else is variable and cannot be directed. I learned to let go of what I thought the return should look like. I let go of everything but my part. I could clearly see that this was the only real way of maintaining a presence of love. I *love*. That is my part. The darkness provided an advanced education in this philosophy. I succeeded. I came through the experience with my love, my truth, and my worthiness.

The Stock Tank Miracle showed me the one and only response to love is love.

While on the drive back out of Hood Canal, Magnus was stating his resistance to what he saw at the time as "the burden of relationships." His eyes were fixed and fierce. There was a gray tint to them that seemed to me to be the shadow of his beliefs. I was raw and done pretending. I was riding along as wounded Mary, saddened by loss and hopeless. I looked over at him and said, "You know? I never asked you to love me. But you won't even accept the love I have to offer you." In that moment we happened to be driving along the beautiful canal with white-capped waters and the Olympic Peninsula as a backdrop. We were just then passing under a bridge, on a narrowing curve. That bridge, that moment, the surrender, all of it is still as vivid today as it was when Magnus looked at me for the first time during this process. Right before me, his eyes turned from a dull gray to as blue as the water. He asked, "You mean I am not responsible for you?" I said, "No, not at all." And once again I meant it. I felt that statement through my spirit. All the relationships in my past I had secretly hoped would complete me. But I knew I could trust within myself that I was worthy of love and love was who I am. It wasn't something I obtained or I could lose. And that freed Magnus of the burden of love. It was a new day. He was introduced to his concept of enoughness. And I had passed my final exam of the heart.

This was only the beginning of breaking the wire woven tightly around our hearts. We saw clearly our beliefs about performance and unworthiness. Before this moment, Magnus felt he had nothing left to give. He felt depleted. With the possibility of unconditioned love, he began to breathe, to see some light. Learning that he could receive love without the strings attached offered him a sense of acceptance for himself that he had not yet recognized in his lifetime. Magnus found his own release. Nothing more was being asked of him. He began to realize his inner sense of worthiness. He was free. The dawn had come after the dark night of the soul.

Whether it is in a horse or a human, acceptance is the mother of worthiness. The remainder of the six-hour drive was spent speaking from our hearts about our pain, our fears, and our hopes. We purged in a sense, opening the chained and barbed shackles that had held us back from worthiness for so long. We talked and talked and talked some more as if no one had ever before heard our voices. This day was only the beginning. On this day along Hood Canal, we began again. We saw that love is indeed real. Our worthiness was rekindled.

All of those lessons from Ray laid the groundwork for my deeper understanding of love. I had to keep offering and have the willingness to set it up and wait. I also had the chance to use enough to be effective. And without a doubt it was so simple it was intensely difficult. All life teaches us about worthiness, because that is what "life" is. It couldn't be any other way. My practice with the horses showed me in unmistakable terms the power and freedom of honoring one's self and another. Just as we can't stop the rain—nor would we benefit by doing so—we can learn to allow the world its way and perfect our own nature in the process. The "heart" of the matter remains untarnished by the storms of life. The lessons can feel extreme. Caving into a belief that our love is conditional only separates us from our natural resource. The grass, the horse, and the man all possess equal worth. Our value is *in* ourselves and *to* one another. Our worth is essential, indispensable, and central to the whole of our experience.

It is within my own mind that I learn to shift my focus from proving my value to realizing it. My wealth lives in my heart, not in an external condition.

I cannot give what I don't believe. I cannot see a loving world while feeling hostility. It is within my own mind that I learn to shift my focus from proving my value to realizing it. My wealth lives in my heart, not in an external condition. Pain can be the bearer of this knowledge if I learn to listen to it. Just as Ray could not teach this, he could only make us aware of it; I retain the responsibility for my own understanding. Recognizing worthiness in all life and not differentiating based on cast or creed opens the true value of love to be expressed honestly and poetically. What greater worth is there on earth? Worthiness is life; it is to be experienced and expressed.

CHAPTER TEN

Resurrection

INALLY WINTER HAS YIELDED ITS HAND TO SPRING, though not without a fight. The transition is a little like a battle between dark and light, with charcoal skies giving way to sun-kissed clouds bursting with the call to life. Rain-soaked fields wield brand-new shoots exploding with every ray of light. Oregon rain is a drenching rain. It seeps into our veins. And just about the time that we feel submerged, it drains to reveal a brand-new world. From the seemingly ceaseless mud is born a blanket of green. The swallows come back to raise their young in their inherited homes, while geese find fields of plenty as marshes subside into grass and grain.

The long, wet winter reluctantly loosens its grip, but not without claiming its dues. I leave a little of myself behind when I wake into the spring. I am a new person; I have learned and lived and left behind an outdated state of mind. I know things this spring that I never knew before. I see with a vision that has been claimed through the passing of time. Time is a great teacher to us all. I welcome a new season with so much more reason and wisdom that I claimed from my pain. Much like birth in physical form, life is claimed through painful passage. The heart, too, seems to pay a price for its glorified release. This winter a part of my life died and then was reborn again in light. This is what resurrection means to me, and with it I am free to see what had been hidden from my sight.

One of the most profound messages Ray Hunt left me with was, "You have to give something you have never given to have something you've never had." In life there are some things I just won't give up. My horses fall into that category. I marry them with a commitment to stand by them in sickness and in health. They are a large part of my chosen family. With that said, they have seen me through all of life's changes. From changing homes and careers to relationships, my horses have remained true. They are that part of my life I call my island, my rock.

The matriarch of the herd I jokingly called my firstborn. Cayenne and I were together for twenty-five years, nearly half my life. She was my teacher, my daughter, my friend, my partner, and most of all, my sage of unconditional love. The trails we traveled spiraled down life's perilous road to find our paths joined forever, not only through life but also through death. She is what brought the lesson of giving what (I felt) I couldn't give, and in turn offered what I never had—the conceptual understanding of resurrection.

It was a crisp fall day in the canyon, with morning chores and the freedom of my diverse lifestyle. I saw my husband off early, before the dawn, then I moved to the barn to run the horses out from their cozy accommodations. I threw a bale of hay onto the mud-strewn four-wheeler and plowed through the ruts in the soggy soil to feed the herd in the field. My gelding Far Go always runs alongside in perfect, balanced form. I never know if this show of athleticism is for my benefit or that of the herd. I guess it just feels good to him to run along beside me. I marveled at the accuracy he had navigating the terrain—unlike me, bulldozing my way across at full speed just to keep from getting stuck. Finally up on higher ground, I stopped and made my daily offering to my masters. People often say to me, "You have horses?" My reply is always, "In truth, they have me."

I love to sit on the four-wheeler in the middle of the herd as they all graze around me. This early morning ritual fills my soul. I see a lot of life in these precious moments, watching the changing weather, seeing the horses in their element, noticing how they feel, and perhaps doing a bit of mothering too. The youngest, Poco, likes to eat the grains of seed left from the hay on the deck of the four-wheeler. That is the one place he knows the older horses won't run him off. As for me, all geared up in my rain suit, mud speckled from head to toe, I, too, am in my element. This is where I belong. This is where my heart lives.

I noted each horse, especially the older mares, for how they moved or sounded when they ate. Cayenne, being the lead mare, got her pick of the piles. No one challenged her. Her reign as queen had never been compromised. Cayenne had seen her share of hardship. As a young horse, she acquired a respiratory ailment called heaves. I particularly listened to her breathing. At twenty-five years old, she had some good days and bad days. In spite of a bit of arthritis in some joints and a tendon issue, she still had grace and spunk! Nonetheless, I kept a watchful eye. She had entered semiretirement but still loved teaching children. This day she had a sixteen-year-old girl who adored her coming for a lesson. I knew this gave both the girl and Cayenne a lift of spirit that could only happen through mutual admiration. I let her eat and enjoy the morning with the herd before coming back to fetch her for the lesson.

As I led Cayenne in from the field, I noticed a very odd movement of her hind leg. She was swinging it out and wide around her. In all my years of having horses, this was new to me. She wasn't limping and didn't seem in pain; it was just how she placed it that was odd. I questioned using her for the lesson that day and thought it was too late to cancel; the girl and her mom were already on their way. I saddled and rode her around to test her out, and I could definitely feel it, but she seemed stable enough. I decided to go ahead with the lesson but with caution. I explained to the girl that part of having animals is being keenly aware of how they feel. They don't tell us when they are sick; we have to be vigilant. As soon as the girl and her mother left, I called the vet.

Since it wasn't an emergency, the vet came the next day. I was relieved that Cayenne showed no signs of pain. I wasn't too alarmed, though it looked to me to be a neurological symptom. The unknown in and of itself created some concern. It can be a challenge for me not to catastrophize when I don't know the answers. I gave myself a pep talk and thought, *We have been through a lot together, Cayenne and I. I will take a deep breath and hope for the best.*

The Best

Sometimes the best is not the ideal. Sometimes the best is about finding the silver lining in the dark clouds. Sometimes the best involves a lot of pain. Fall mornings in Oregon can be cold, dark, and wet. This time can also be like Eden. Bright, clear skies lend a crisp, clean air that vitalizes, tantalizes, and mesmerizes one's spirit. After a dry, busy summer, we Oregonians often love the opportunity to cozy up and nest. Nature seems to make this transition seamlessly. Whether it is a dry year or a wet year, the hottest on record or the coldest, nature knows how to adjust to change and diversity. She doesn't seem to judge it as good or bad. Daily life tries to mimic nature with all its highs and lows. The degrees between heaven and hell can be found right inside our minds.

The experience with Cayenne that I was beginning to embrace offered within it all of the mind's polarities. I found despair and joy. I found the deepest of connections as well as my fear of separation. I found illness, and I found triumph over it. I found hope and hopelessness. In this one life experience, I experienced all of life. From that day in the pasture when Cayenne first started to show symptoms and in the four months following, I was taught about not only the preciousness of life but also the uncertainty of death. Yes, the uncertainty of death. I found that death, too, was in my mind. And if it was in my mind, I had the power to understand it.

Sometimes the best is not the ideal. Sometimes the best is about finding the silver lining in the dark clouds. Sometimes the best involves a lot of pain.

I wanted to give Cayenne the best of everything I had to give. Of course that meant keeping the vet close at hand and offering supplements from A to Z and anti-inflammatory, pain-reducing drugs. But deep in my heart I knew what seemed to be most important to Cayenne was that I dedicated my thoughts, my prayers, and my hopes for her recovery and to our relationship. The best for Cayenne was certainly not limited to her physical needs. It was love that she really drank in. It was love that broke the barrier of helplessness we both seemed to be experiencing. I was never at a loss when I realized that I could be with her in a deeply spiritual way. This was how we began to transcend the illness.

Cayenne experienced miraculous moments both emotionally and physically. For instance, after days of not eating, all at once her appetite returned and she ate voraciously. Or when she had been staggering like a drunken sailor and then miraculously walked, balanced and beautiful. In addition, she opted to trot at liberty, then loped a perfect circle in a collected canter. One day

I remember the intense joy I experienced when she insisted on rejoining the herd. I drove out on the four-wheeler to check on her, and all the horses circled around me. It was as if we were celebrating the return of their matriarch. I could feel the herd's unity, and Cayenne was in the middle of it. I experienced the warmth of family while sitting and breathing in this precious moment. This was "the best."

I was determined to be present. My best was my presence. I learned to be right where she was, not where I wished she would be. In being present with Cayenne in every phase of her journey, I found that I could also be present in mine. The one repeated declaration I made to her became the one message that helped me transcend my perception of death itself. Each and every day I would say to her, "I will never leave you." This I made a solemn vow. At times when she faltered and I feared the illness would take her life, I spoke of riding in the clouds. I spoke to her of freedom and of a bond that could not be severed.

The peaks and valleys continued throughout winter. There were a handful of times when I believed she might not make it through the night, then the following day she would rally and return with courageous determination. In late January I began to see some signs that led me to understand that there were serious internal conditions that appeared to be advancing. One morning I went into the arena where she had been resting and found an enormous amount of blood in the sand. The vet was called, and we did an ultrasound to find she had fluid in her abdomen. The cause of Cayenne's illness remained a mystery. Unfortunately, there was no doubt that it was worsening.

Cayenne was self-medicating. I turned her out on lush green grass, and she opted to eat the nearby blackberries. She seemed to intuitively know what resources she had that might help her. I researched medicinal uses of blackberry and found there were many. The benefits included antioxidants, fiber, and everything from support of the immune system to the healing of wounds. It seemed Cayenne knew what she needed much more than I did. So I cut a pickup load of blackberries and made sure she had access to them at night in her stall. Then she took to eating bark from the trees. Not any bark, only the fir trees. This, too, was shown to have healing factors when I researched it. Cayenne had an incredible awareness of treatment, and I followed her lead. I found myself watching every move she made. Cayenne's health became my mission.

One rainy, cold night I was greatly concerned. She had been out with the herd, and when I called the horses into the barn for the night, she didn't come in with them. It was just dusk, and my heart pounded as I ran as fast as I could to the far edge of the pasture, where I found her under a tree. She had moved off by herself, and this was unlike her. My heart collapsed in fear as I approached. With rain starting and nightfall upon us, I had to get her to the barn about four hundred yards away. I haltered her and asked her to move, and she resisted. I pleaded as the rain came down, and she stepped slowly for about a hundred feet and stopped. I was alone, and my mind raced as I tried to devise a plan to get her back to the barn. She would rest and then start again. Eventually we made it. I left most of the remainder of the hope I had in the field that night.

When the rain pounds on the tin roof of the barn and all the horses are tucked in eating their hay under the soft lights, there is a sense of warmth and contentment that permeates the space. Sometimes I sit out there just to feel the sense of relief and fulfillment at the end of a winter day. On this night, after bringing Cayenne in on a wing and a prayer, the relief was unsurpassed. On this night I just couldn't bring myself to leave her. I decided to set up camp. Magnus helped me with all the provisions for a comfortable night, right down to a heated blanket and a thermos of hot tea. I parked my lounge chair in the aisle just outside her stall and left her door open so I could be near her. Cayenne left her night's feed to come and stand beside me. With her hind foot cocked, she was safe and warm and resting.

As I listened to the pelting rain, I closed my eyes and lost myself in a deep meditation. In this endless, vast spaciousness of my heart, I encountered the same in Cayenne. I was embracing the relationship in the pure essence of spirit. What came next was more valuable than words can describe. And perhaps the story may get lost here in translation. In this timeless moment there was no human and no horse, no illness and no fear, no gap that separates and divides, only love. This love had one descriptive term that seemed to penetrate not only my awareness but also my entire mind—my soul, if you will. It wasn't a word but an experience. I can roughly describe it as joy. It was not the joy that we know in some material realm but spiritual joy, the kind that knows no opposite. The mind cannot understand things that have no opposite. The mind must label all it knows, and it does this by comparing. The spiritual joy I experienced was beyond my mind. It required no explanation. No words, no label, no understanding, it was simply undeniable. It was total, complete, and lacking nothing; it was union and communion. I knew in this surreal moment I had experienced knowledge, truth, and exactly what I had taken birth for. I couldn't have planned it, learned it, bought it, or made it. It made me.

The Message

What I experienced that dark and blustery night in early February left me dangling to understand the edgy border between life and death. Though I had no idea what was to come next, I see now that timeless moment of connection, beyond anything I could rationally understand, was to be my beacon for the remainder of the life lessons my Cayenne would teach me. Still, even on this day as I write, the message of deep, spiritual joy is the underlay to my life. Returning to this joy is the message in each meditation, prayer, and call for love I make.

In this timeless moment there was no human and no horse, no illness and no fear, no gap that separates and divides, only love.

What I felt that night is what I feel this journey we call life is all about. There is a call in us all to return home to this unconditioned sense of peace: life without fear, a joy that knows no death—no end. This is what I felt in that timeless instant while connecting so deeply to the horse that had been my constant, my friend, and my teacher. She was still offering lessons way beyond what is of the mind. This was the lesson the heart teaches, and she had my full attention. That night I felt what is beyond death and fear and illness. Now I know I can reach for that freedom from fear again and again.

In the weeks to come, I wandered through the world of unknown destiny. All that I knew was love, and that, I knew, was certain. One day after giving Cayenne a long massage, I sat (as I often did) on the stage at the end of the arena. I love this perch. When I sit there the horses can stand beside me and we are comfortably eye-to-eye. On this afternoon, Cayenne had her nose nestled in my lap. I read aloud from one of my treasured books, *Embracing the Beloved* by Stephen and Ondrea Levine. It was a meditation on healing. One verse resonated deeply in my heart:

This connection is so powerful. Don't think it, be it.
Let it in. Let it in.
Let yourself be loved that much. Let it in. Have mercy
on you.
Let your pain be touched by mercy and loving kindness.
Let it in.

I wanted Cayenne to feel the pouring of my heart. And yet when I read the words "Let yourself be loved that much," I realized how hard that was for me. This healing was for both of us. We were, as we had been throughout our lives, in it together. I saw clearly my need for healing in my desire for hers. This was often what came from the teachings of my horse-to-human intimacy. I thought I was teaching her, and all the while she was teaching me. In this interplay I felt my own sense of loss. I realized that I had been so driven by her pain that I had left my own in the field that day, four months earlier, when I had noticed her awkward stride. I had left Mary. How could I be truly present with her if I was not present with myself? This was a missing link—and a very important one.

That night the sky was clear, but my mind wasn't. The night air was cold and crisp, and I opted to leave the rest of the herd out for the night. Cayenne came into the corral, and I saw a different look in her eye. One I had not seen before. As I closed the door to the stall, both her eyes locked onto mine, and she leaned through the window of the stall door. She was asking me to stay. I felt it. I opened the door, went back in, and wrapped my arms around her neck. Chest to chest, I cried and repeated what I had said every day of this experience: "I will never leave you." I still feel the sensation of our two hearts as I held on for dear life. I mean that literally. I held on to this life and was hell-bent not to let go. Her eyes that night still call to me. I see them in my dreams. This look was the only real difference about her. She did not seem distressed, other than wanting me close. The herd was just outside the corral, and they could visit over the fence. I reluctantly went inside to sleep.

There is a moment in early morning when the sleeping world wakes, when just a glimmer of light from the sun breaks through the darkness of night. I never tire of this moment; in fact, it fills me with awe. The birds seem to embrace the new day with joy as well. It's as if they sing for sheer speculation of a great new beginning. Life is a consistent teacher, and a good one. The cycles repeat as if to tell us, "Look, this is how it is." Day follows night—it never falters. Why then do we tend to believe in endings?

Day follows night—it never falters. Why then do we tend to believe in endings?

I couldn't wait to check on Cayenne. The first light of day had not yet come, and the birds were still silent. I entered the corral with medicine and supplements in hand. I gave her a healthy dose of vitamins and a bit of pain medication to help her through the day. She took it as she always did with grace and patience. I noticed there wasn't a horse in sight, which was very unusual. Mornings are feeding time, and they tend to stay close to the barn. I opened the gate and let Cayenne out to wander down toward the arena. By the time she got to the end of the fence line, about a hundred feet away, I realized something was very, very different. I ran down and wrapped my arms around her and instinctively asked if I should get Far Go (her adopted son). The answer was clear: "No!" It was a cold, clear morning with damp, melting frost. I wasn't dressed warmly enough to stay with her too long. I decided to run to the house and put on some gear so that I could stay near as long as need be.

While I was in the house, I felt a literal shove from behind. There is no easy way to describe this, but perhaps it was as if there was a gale force pushing me, an invisible pressure. With it I sensed the thought, *Get to the arena now.* I ran as fast as I could back to Cayenne. As I entered the arena, she came to meet me and leaned her whole face into my chest. I knew what was happening. I held her as close to my heart as I could and said, "I want your freedom, my love." The words from the meditation the day before came streaming into my mind. With tears flowing, I cried, "Please, allow yourself to be loved that much."

After holding Cayenne's head within my arms and pleading for her release, she stepped away and walked a full lap around the edge of the arena. Her entire hide was vibrating. I had no idea what to expect. It is my honest feeling that this vibration was her spirit leaving the body, yet her body made it all the way around the building to the door of the tack room. The tack room is where we spent many wonderful moments together. There on the wall hangs a favorite picture of Ray Hunt grinning his infectious grin. This is where she chose to let go. I dropped to my knees to pray, and Cayenne dropped to her knees to sleep. I held her head in my lap as she galloped across the invisible bridge that lies between a life in form and spiritual freedom.

After what seemed to be an endless instant, a time neither short nor long but surreal in its oddity, I looked up from my imploding realm of altered states to see once again. The sun was up and the birds were singing. It was beautiful in its ceaselessness to be. My mind was shattered, but my heart stood still to hear the song of this new day. Then I turned around, and on the hillside behind me, in perfect stillness, stood the entire herd.

Each one of the horses stood in a different place in the trees, each one standing hauntingly still. They didn't move a foot or eat a blade of grass. Each horse focused intently on their friend, their leader, their teacher, their herd mate. Not a sound was made throughout this silent vigil. The horses didn't move from their stance for nearly an hour.

Reverse Reality

As I walked away from the arena that early February morning, I walked away from the Mary that I was when I woke up that day. I walked away from a sense of control. I realized my false sense of stability was like a widow-maker in the woods, a fallen tree leaning on a healthy one. My thoughts about what life is were as dependent on circumstance and equally as unstable. We don't want to think we have no control. We want to believe in the rut our mind has carved out for us. We want to lean on the safety of its confining walls. When we experience a mind-shattering event, the shards of broken pieces fall in such disarray as to insist we rearrange our thoughts to accommodate a new perspective.

The moments after experiencing a death can feel a little like returning to land after an ocean voyage. The equilibrium is skewed, and solid ground feels unstable. The real world looks to be a dream, and the dreamlike state of shock seems very real. There is a reverse reality that can take place.

These moments, after witnessing my beloved Cayenne's body conclude its journey, presented a crossroads to my awareness of what it means to be alive. I began to question the validity of life. If it was this fragile, with only death as its destination, was it as real as I had always believed it to be? And what of the love and of the relationship to love that inspired this joyful journey?

My relationship with Cayenne did not die when she did. It has no end, nothing tangible to wither and return to dust. What could not be seen with the body's eyes is very real, and what could be touched by the senses disappears as fast as a magician's illusion. The dichotomy of this paradox was blurring a lifelong belief. I believed that life was physical. I felt that our expressions, creations, and relationships in life were a by-product of the life we lived. But what became hauntingly clear on that crisp, new day was just the opposite. What I see in the physical world is expression. The inner relationship (which I call love) is what everlasting life truly is. This is the meaning of resurrection. Life must be everlasting. Life can't be death; the two are opposed realities.

This is the meaning of resurrection. Life must be everlasting. Life can't be death; the two are opposed realities.

Horses consistently teach me that what I think I know to be true typically isn't. We are so sure of things: our identity, our relationships, our perspective. Yet these perceptions are but echoes of a past that is not at all present. The labels we learned to pin on our lives stick to our vision like lint to wool. Do we question our thoughts as we grow into new dimensions? Are we investing our minds into what is truly real?

When a horse guides me to answer a question I ponder, the answer is most often completely reverse of what I had originally thought was fact. But frankly, if I knew the truth, I wouldn't be looking for an answer in the first place. The altered state of shocking grief casts a view into a world we're not likely to visit—the world of a reverse reality. When our minds can scarcely contain the pain of a loss so great, we are forced to look for answers to questions we have never asked. The question I asked in grief was, How do I keep my promise "I will never leave you"? How do I follow Cayenne into a world I cannot see, touch, or experience with my body?

The answer revealed itself months later: I don't follow Cayenne. The answer led me to understand it is I who is lost, and in fact, it is Cayenne who will never leave me.

In this world we see form and think it is real, and we see love and think it is imagined, fragile, elusive, or temporary. We see each other and feel separate. This is the greatest illusion of all.

I have often said, "Fear is not logical; it is biological." So if life (bio) includes death as part of its system, it is a living contradiction to truth. Truth cannot change and still be truth. The experience I embraced within a deep and loving relationship led me to see that my life is not what I do. A teacher once said, "If you are what you do, then if you don't, you aren't." We tend to believe what we are taught by others who were taught that life is a series of doings. When Ray Hunt used the term *life*, I grasped that he was speaking to the spirit. A horse with a lot of life was one that had energy and ambition and was truly a horse. That is what I am saying here as well. Life is not something we see; it is something we are. When I deeply experienced the death of a body, I came to know that life has no end...no death.

Resurrection Is Freedom from Death

To unknot the common but untrue mind-set that the body's senses are "cause" rather than "effect" is a large undertaking; I am simply stating potential here. Fully embracing the truth in resurrection has been identified in spiritual texts for all millennia. By sharing my journey into the heart and heat of humanness

and identifying the optional paths that lead to a very nonconventional recovery, I hope to portray that we need not settle for
feelings of loss and hopelessness. We will indeed experience
them, but my point is we don't have to settle for the end. There
is no end. This is the premise of this book. Perfect practice is
not settling for death. It is not settling for what is not nirvana.
What does life have to do with death?

CHAPTER ELEVEN

The Do-Over

AFTER A LONG NIGHT AND A HARD RAIN, THE MORNING can glow with a rare and wondrous sight, a clear and crystalline light. This special kind of light is crisp and fresh. It paints the landscape with a tint of red and gold that resembles a burning ember. Light like this radiates and pulsates; it is not stagnant or passive like the harsh summer sun. This light commands my attention, and this morning it had it.

When seasons cycle through and characteristics of a seldom-seen (yet familiar) light return, I have the chance to reflect on all the changes I have made in my life. I see the attributes of a life well lived. I see my heart's capacity grow. I see my painful history fading behind me as I emerge anew and refreshed. I have earned my view of this clear and radiant light. I have stayed the storms that have offered a greater understanding of my deepest purpose. Staying the storm isn't for everyone. Many find it just too painful to look deeply into life's process. Change, at times, can cause chaos in an organized, well-defined life. It is easy to be fearful of change because change can stir up feelings that might have been neatly tucked away. Staying the storm does not mean enduring life; it means inquiring into it.

Fear follows challenge as a bitter aftertaste. It takes something sweet to tolerate the sour. Staying the storm provides the sweetness, the unmistakable nectar of success. I'm not comfortable leaving trouble without learning from its lessons. I devoutly believe that hidden deep within the very trouble that finds its way to me is the knowledge that I came into this life to learn. This certainly does not mean I go out looking for trouble. It means I aim to make sense of the storms of my experience. The crystalline light that guides me is buried deep within the storms of my life. There, at the convergence of my mind and the metaphorical weather, is the offering and my purpose. If I refuse to navigate, to see inside the eye of it, I lose the opportunity of what it has to teach me and all that those lessons offer.

A do-over is what I call re-riding the line, or getting a second chance to make things right. It's my way of healing a past pain or righting a wrong. Ray would sometimes mention this when he shared that we can't expect to ride through something bad and come out good. But he also taught us to accept defeat to gain success. The do-over is my way of blending these ideas.

Life hands us experiences—sometimes they are less than desirable. Sometimes they come like that, and sometimes we just mess things up. My regrets are only lessons I have yet to master. My relationships with horses and with people are of the greatest value to me. They are also what motivates me most to learn from my past. I am always learning and growing, and I sure don't know what I know until I know it. Often, even when I think I know something, I find out I don't know the real truth about it. The real truth, or meaning, is the hidden gem. Healing my relationships is the most significant work I can do.

I heard Ray say, "I wish I knew then what I think I know now." He knew that knowledge evolved over time. He was a student, as good as, or better than, any one of us. He was always willing to find another way—a better way, a way that was more efficient or simplistic. He'd encourage us endlessly to do less to gain more. These are the attributes of educated learners.

The ones who don't settle, who know they don't know. This is where true brilliance abides.

Leaving in Love

When an experience has left a less than desirable outcome lingering in my mind, the memory of it haunts me until I eventually set up the do-over. I see life as an education. And if I am to learn how to live well, I need to understand my mistakes and do right by them. This is a basic principle to advance in any curriculum. If I don't set up the do-over, the powers that be will. I know that whether it's my horse, my relationships, or my education, if I leave pain in the past, I will have to return to live it again. This is the curriculum of life. We repeat to resolve.

My regrets are only lessons I have yet to master.

Resolving conflict doesn't always mean that we live happily ever after. Sometimes resolution is letting go of pain through a peaceful process. Just as letting go by running away in fear can create more fear, letting go with love can create more love. I found this to be true as I experienced a powerful process while in my forties. I had a long-term relationship with a man I loved very much. Neither one of us was very well equipped to lean into our pain or resolve conflict. But we did indeed love each other. At the time, my mother was suffering from the early onset of dementia, and I was focused on helping her into a peaceful living environment. I finally found a suitable treatment center for my mom and admitted her there. Shortly thereafter she had a sudden cardiac tamponade and died quite unexpectedly. This painful process took me away from the much-needed focus on my failing relationship. As it happened, I was unaware that my partner had reached out to another woman for support and approval. A few weeks later I noticed some suspicious calls made late in the night on the cell phone bill I shared with my boyfriend. I asked him if he was involved with another woman. He admitted openly that he was. When he told me this, I realized that I did not have the capacity to save my relationship and grieve my mother simultaneously. I told him that I loved him very much and that I hoped he would bring the love that we shared into his next relationship. I could see that I had left him long before we actually split up.

The beauty and the wisdom from this story is that I still feel love in my heart all these years later. I let go in love; I did not let go in fear. So love is what lingered. This is one example of how powerful our ability to love truly is. It also taught me that resolution doesn't always mean staying in a situation. But it did require a peaceful process of release. My pain from unresolved conflicts shows up in my perceptions of fear, doubt, unworthiness, and sorrow. I don't want to settle for these traits in myself or in my horse. When I have resolution, the pain's purpose is complete. Resolution is how I develop right-mindedness and right vision. My way of seeing is dependent on my way of being. Oftentimes, with horses or with humans, where you leave something is right where you'll pick it up. Knowing this, I won't settle for less than bliss. This is, for me, the pathway of evolution and the premise for this book. I am not here to park. Settling has never come easy for me. Learning and growing and expanding are essential for my well-being.

Healing in a Storm

A rainstorm off the coast was rapidly heading inland, with winds powerful enough to cause damage. For me the damage had already been done. I was heading into this storm to heal. And the powers that be were asking (as they often do), How badly do you want it?

That God, what a kidder. The storm of storms hit the mainland the day of our departure. It was four thirty in the morning, and Magnus and I were driving south on Interstate 5. I had signed up for the first away clinic since I had made my fearful escape at the clinic in Washington three years prior. This clinic was a large do-over for me. The rainstorm was symbolic of the one I was facing inside my mind. This inner storm was my historical blunder—that past experience from which I recoiled in remembering. It was time to re-ride the line, to take my second chance, my do-over. The fear of failure had festered long enough.

This departure into the storm of storms challenged my resolve within the first hour. I was determined to prevail. I would no longer live with the pain of my guilt. The process Magnus and I had endured on our trip up Hood Canal still generated heat in the cells of my memory. We had resolved our resistance. But our process, at the time, had overshadowed the guilt I felt having left Far Go tied when he was reeling from his own trauma. I never had turned loose of my regret that I had left him in his moment of need. I felt terrible that he had paid a price for my awakening. The regret combined with the way I had left that clinic—running away, feeling depleted and defeated—left fear festering in my mind. I knew I wouldn't settle for fear; it's against all that I believe in. I just wasn't quite sure when or how my do-over would evolve. It seemed the time had come. My silent mental anguish had me questioning my own character and that of the world in which I live. I was ready to change all that, and I was strong enough to face my fears again. After all, it's never too late to try, even if we try simply within our own mind.

I left this piece of my past in mental anguish. Guilt has a penetrating blow that acts as acute trauma to the identity—a jolt that rattles the bones. I had already extracted tremendous wealth of self from this past experience. Magnus and I had broken our false paradigms of what love is. That was essential, and that alone was worth the pain. But there was more to do. I wanted freedom from the past, from that image of Far Go tied up. I wouldn't settle for leaving it in regret. I had been hosting clinics at our place throughout those years in between, but it was time to head out into the world again. I had one goal: absolute dedication and commitment to my lifelong partner Far Go. This was our do-over. I wouldn't settle for less than a unified approach. This willingness held my release.

Guilt has a penetrating blow that acts as acute trauma to the identity—a jolt that rattles the bones.

My horses seem to patiently accept my blunderings and forgive the time it takes for me to learn and grow. Both Ray and Tom reminded us that it sometimes takes a full lifetime to learn to live a lifetime. I'm not sure if I had ever felt the sting of this kind of personal guilt in my relationship with my horses. My horses tend to come first in my life. I am willing to sacrifice myself for their well-being. But during this particular challenge, I was so lost I had nothing to draw from. I was deeply humbled. I reminded myself of Ray's comforting words so many years ago, when I felt at fault; he had told me that sometimes I might have to go in and have my breakfast and take a fresh start. The guilt prompted a nagging need to revisit the feelings I had at that clinic, and to do it with my horse. The do-over seemed like a long-overdue fresh start.

Now with white knuckles in a black night, I was driving

down the interstate with an inner state of disbelief. That age-old question rising long before the morning light: *Really, Mary? Is growth worth the risk?* Doubt has a voice of its own. I've come to learn that this voice is not me; it's my past talking. Somehow, I suppose, all the outdated thoughts I acquired long ago see my need for resolution as a death sentence. These doubts need my attention to live. I need their release to flourish. In this way we are mutually exclusive.

Growth is worth the pain; it has to be. Otherwise we just endure pain without purpose. Rainwater was flooding the highway. The windshield was opaque with the tidal splash offered by passing long-haul trucks. I remembered my quest. I reminded myself that my greatest accomplishments came through the storms of conflict.

I aimed my one-ton dually toward the next highway exit then continued past it to the next, and so on down the road we went—just like how I've inched my way through most perils in my life. *Don't look too far beyond where you are. Small increments of success.* And certainly, *Don't look down, keep your eye on the ball. Steady as she goes.* The self-talk talked me through it, but all the while with the permission to turn back if I so chose.

My horse came along as a willing hostage, alone with his own thoughts in a darkened trailer on a stormy highway. No one asked him to choose. He just trusts. He trusts that I won't take him somewhere he can't handle. Once again I take my lead from him, knowing my heart is led by a source who seems to have a higher opinion of my capabilities than I do. I trust this source like my horse trusts me. Blind admiration, I suppose.

Horses have one up on us. They have an innate ability to stay present with all and only what is happening now. If I were to think about riding in the do-over clinic with the predicted winds powerful enough to peel the metal from the building, I most likely would have just buckled. One town at a time passed through my rearview mirror until we finally arrived in Junction City, Oregon.

In my restless dream of resolution, I felt determined to find my peace of mind, the part of me that I had left behind when I ran away in fear. Looking at my pain, I realized so much of it came from a sense of unworthiness—not an intellectually determined statement but more of a long, unconscious decaying of my sense of self. It was that dull, seeping feeling of not-enoughness. For three years I carried the burden of trepidation. It was now time to join my past experience with my present wisdom and bring it forward with the intention to heal.

It was now time to join my past experience with my present wisdom and bring it forward with the intention to heal.

For decades my altars have been horse barns. The one we would call home for this particular weekend was simple and sufficient but placed in a wide-open field with little blockage from the impending weather. The barn looked a bit the way I felt, vulnerable and exposed. It was 8:00 a.m. sharp when we pulled in the driveway. As fate would have it, the clouds eased apart for a glimpse at the sun, a momentary break before the next squall. Just enough time for me to get Far Go saddled and get to the arena.

This break in the weather felt validating, comforting, and a bit symbolic. With the first difficulty behind us, we earned this pause. One important aspect of the do-over is the advantage of contrast. When I mindfully return to the challenge, I am much more aware. When I feel that I have been hurt in the past, I have a heightened sense of vigilance. By contrast, the moments of relief and breakthrough feel far better than I ever imagined them to be. I really appreciate the good times. This became very evident on this do-over trip. If I had just loaded my horse in pleasant weather and found a perfectly safe place to land, I might not have gained the real depth of value that the contrasting emotions offered. The storm was a viable part of the success.

The second trial was soon to follow. As I entered the barn, I met an old friend and another unresolved sorrow: the fear of rejection. I felt a tightening of my chest and a bristling of my breath. To be honest, this fear probably developed in me around the age of eight, when I was just a little girl in school. School was a brutal place for me, and I acquired a real deep sense of defensiveness. We all know the pain (in one form or another) of judgment, separation, and feeling left out. Grade-school kids can be ruthless with words, and it seemed I gave them plenty to talk about.

I fought hard against what seemed, to my eight-year-old ego, to be the wrongful judgment by others. It was as if at the age of eight my world became unfriendly. I questioned who I was. The opinions of my teachers and peers didn't fit with the vision I held of myself. Other people's ridicule began clinging to my mind and penetrating my not-yet-hardened heart. This paradox would, in time, influence who I would become. Third grade was my introduction to dualism. It was when I learned about the "us versus them" mentality. Therein lies the great debate: who I was and who they thought me to be.

The tender years of my early childhood development were when these wounds burrowed into the weave of my psyche. Without notice, I formed opinions about other people's opinions and developed a belief of invalidation. These frightening ideas of insecurity and the false judgments by others are what initiate feelings of separation and defensiveness. They are subtle in their ways. These thoughts are completely unsubstantiated and provocative. They are the whispers in my mind—*I am different, I will never fit in*—reminding me I am unloved and unlovable. Trial number two was the mirror of exclusion.

Clinics, like high school, are composed of individuals coming together to make a group. I attend a clinic because I want to learn from my teacher and bond with my horse. This is my main objective. There is, however, another aspect to clinics, a certain sociological climate. Groups are formed, and a social network is built. I had attended clinics for decades and had yet to find a group to "belong" to. Not fitting into groups was a big part of my early education. This did not change when I traded an academic education for an equestrian one. When I entered the barn, there to meet me were the ghosts of clinics past.

Seeing my friend that morning brought back all the feelings from the uncomfortable end to our longtime relationship. Throughout the years, I had invited this friend to attend all the clinics I arranged. I felt surprised and disappointed when I learned that I was no longer welcome to join the gatherings that she hosted. This sudden change in our relationship concerned me. As soon as I became aware of it, I reached out to see if I had offended her. I conveyed my disappointment, though our conversation did not reveal the cause. I never knew what happened, and I went on to feel the pain of rejection.

Of course I realize it is not being excluded from her group that hurts so much. It is simply the historic pain of exclusion. Seeing her as I walked through the door of my do-over clinic seemed profound. I responded as I always did with a warm smile and an outstretched hand. I was surprisingly relieved as I walked away. The contrast again offered me peace. I remembered I was here for the horse. I felt a wave of joy for that unwavering bond. There was a real distinction of value in that moment. I felt Far

Go with me more than ever. And I didn't want to be anywhere but where we were.

I found the best antidote for exclusion is inclusion. Ray had a phrase that made me smile to think of it: "Whistle, grin, and ride." This is good medicine, and what I used as I walked away from my ole friend. With my willingness intact and holding no opinion of other's opinions, I was free to enjoy the clinic. It takes two opinions for debate, so when I focused on what I loved, I would most certainly find inclusion. I loved my horse and my husband. Both were there to settle the rattling of the bones in the closet of my mind. Far Go was noticeably calm, and I couldn't wait to climb into the best seat in the house—my saddle.

I found the best antidote for exclusion is inclusion.

Every ride is different, just like every day is different. Far Go is full of life and holds great pride in his own abilities. He is noble and leads his herd with consistent accuracy. I often think he would have made a spectacular wild horse, and yet I have been graced with his presence all these twenty-plus years. Having raised him from a colt, I have a very special bond with him. There have been times I've had no idea how to help him, and countless more, I am sure, he felt the same about me. I have had Far Go in situations where I felt his hide vibrate in fear, yet somehow he holds it all together. He and I are a lot alike. We can be deeply sensitive and yet also masters at survival. I see a lot of myself in Far Go.

I was hoping both Far Go and I would recover our composure at this do-over clinic. We were equals in this partnership, and this clinic was as important for him as it was for me. We had one job, and that was to feel good. I aimed to do only what was right for both of us, no matter what. My directive was clear: it was well-being.

As I picked up the reins and we moved across the arena, I felt something that I can scarcely describe. Perhaps the word is *nothing*. I felt nothing in my hands. Far Go was weightless. He felt like silk. The wind was howling, and with barely a thought, I asked to move forward. Smooth acceleration is never better than when the transition from walk to trot cannot be felt. Far Go glided wherever directed and turned with presence. All the riders entered the arena and created a maze of pathways for us to follow. It felt like we were flying, as I could barely feel his feet beneath me. The pounding of the wind on the wall couldn't distract my Far Go from his own state of grace.

I could have gone home in the first five minutes. I felt, in just that much time, everything I came for. I felt unity, forgiveness, acceptance, peace, love…I felt my horse feeling back to me. I knew we'd had our do-over. All was forgiven and left behind on that stormy weekend in Junction City.

As the howling wind increased, I saw the edge of the roof flapping. I wondered if the storm would get intense enough that we would need to evacuate the arena. Wind can be a frightening and unpredictable thing, and a metal roof on a horse barn is not exactly a safe haven. But Far Go stayed present and so did I. I had faith that we would know what to do when we needed to do it. Ray used to talk about the chance that he could get hurt or maimed while working with horses, but then he'd add that it really didn't matter what could happen if it hadn't happened yet. I think about that from time to time when I am worried or scared. What I thought Ray was saying was *Don't buy trouble.* There is no need to see trouble in something that hasn't even happened. I used that windstorm to get closer with my horse than perhaps I had ever been. And guess what—the roof never did peel off.

Throughout the next three days, Far Go and I continued to grow. I could feel that my fears were diminishing and so were my old, outdated assumptions. I had done it. I had leaned into my fears and found peace. The ride on Far Go was one I will never forget. People who attended the clinic and had known us both in the past came to me and said what a great change they saw. I smiled and was grateful for this acknowledgment. But truthfully it would have been equally as fulfilling without it. Although, when I hear others share what they saw in me while in such an experience as this, I sometimes think of it as a message from the powers that be. I see those who share their observations as simply the messengers. Our relationships mirror back to us what we feel and live. I knew that in this clinic I had found my own perfect practice within myself. I had honored the relationship with my horse and with myself, and that was what these folks witnessed. It had very little to do with my riding. Tom would say when finding unity with our horses it might seem like we could "ride them up a telephone pole or down a badger hole." He'd say that we wouldn't do either one, but it would feel as if we could. That's what I felt with Far Go every minute of this clinic. I felt that I could jump over the moon.

There is an aspect in my relationship with horses that is nearly impossible to describe. And I will just touch on it here. When my mind opens and I ride with my heart, I find my horses are waiting right there, at the gateway to meet me. It is as if they know when I am thinking and they know when I am deeply feeling. They respond in suit.

Horses have an incredible intuitive ability to meet us on our own terms. They are a mirror. I think this is why they can be as gentle as lambs with children or can be used as therapy animals. In fact, just last night I witnessed this marvel. I was working with some horses at a barn where I met a woman who had what doctors call a learning deficiency. This woman had had a seizure when she was an infant. She was in a coma for nine days. Her brain was affected, and now as a fifty-year-old woman, she is still very childlike in her mentality. She led a horse into the arena, and I noticed that the horse stayed with her mentally every moment. I was intrigued and consciously observed the relationship. The incredible beauty of this woman is that, having a mind of a child, she sings, laughs, and cries with abandon. I could tell that the horse was completely tuned into her channel. That coma had in no way affected her spirit. In fact, she was leading with her spirit. Because her mind was compromised, her feelings were free to be right on the surface. This horse could sense this; it was evident. I am just guessing, but I think horses can trust feelings. They relate to the honesty, to the authentic nature of feelings.

The old cliché that horses can smell fear may be true, but not for the reasons people think. They are keenly aware of emotions—all emotions. When we, as riders, really open our heart to the ride, so (it seems) does the horse. This is especially true in a partnership where the horse feels a close connection and trust with the human. Far Go and I have shared so many heartfelt experiences. We are connected very deeply because together we have deeply experienced life, and this became profoundly evident that weekend in Junction City. Shared experience is what a relationship is.

My intention for this do-over clinic was to ride with an open heart, to have the relationship be the most important element of the ride. Far Go knew it. And I knew he knew it. And he knew I knew he knew it. The unity I felt was no coincidence; it was intended. I suppose that is the essential teaching of riding into a storm. Diving back in gave me the chance to reclaim what is naturally mine. It gave me the chance to find again what I had sacrificed for fear. It gave me a choice.

I have realized in my life there are only two emotions. Though I have heard many debates on this subject, and of course the "yeah buts…" appear, I see our two choices as love and fear. There are countless words one could use to describe these options. *Love* and *fear* are just the two I choose. Perhaps another term would be *resistance* or *nonresistance*. Either way, all roads lead to one or the other. I learned that how I leave an experience emotionally is what sets up my future perspective. If I leave an experience in a fearful past, I will see from a perspective of fear. It was clear to me on this blustery October weekend that I was leaving this experience in love. Because of that I rewrote the script for my future clinics. I won't settle for fear, not ever.

Raising the Bar

This book is an adventure story about reaching into the deepest parts of me. My life is a series of explorations and adventures leading me home to a greater understanding of what I know to be true. This voyage into perfect practice is about moving my bar; it's about growth, enchantment, and empowerment.

Ray Hunt and Tom Dorrance were both masters at learning. They learned how to improve on the undesirable. It didn't seem to me that they were too keen on settling for what they didn't want. When one is willing to add passion and inspiration to intentions of perfection, the abundance of this world is free to supply its endless options. I greatly improved my life by my willingness to grow. I don't have to settle for a painful past. I can rewrite the script of my life.

Allowing do-overs in all aspects of my life is how I learn forgiveness. The difference between sin and error is that error can be corrected. It is simply sinful if we are unwilling to grow from our pain. I don't really believe that anyone would settle for pain or a painful past if they realized they have a choice. No matter the error, no matter the time lapse, and no matter the outcome, we can choose to change our view. We can change how we see life, and we can evolve our perspective. The do-over can be done on anything, by anyone, at any time. The do-over is forgiveness, acceptance, and love, all of which offer freedom.

When one is willing to add passion and inspiration to intentions of perfection, the abundance of this world is free to supply its endless options.

Far Go and I headed back to our canyon home with our minds full. I opened the trailer door to escort him back to his herd. I knew we both had grown up a little. Still using the opportunity of our "lifetime to learn to live a lifetime," we felt a deep sense of peace. Far Go's herd was nowhere in sight. He had been gone from them for days. In the past he would have been calling out to them—anxious to regain the security the herd offered. But this was a new day with a new way. As I turned him out to rejoin his family, he walked slowly, methodically, his tail gracefully swinging. A gentle breeze and a bit of sun offered a warming welcome. The storm had lifted and so had our hearts.

Chapter Twelve

Don't Shoot the Guru: The Art of Acceptance

Ever since I was a little girl, I wanted to teach. It was one of those things that I said at the age of five long before I even knew what the word meant. Then, as I got to school, I found that I wasn't an academic. I was experiential. I enjoyed exploring and learning about life, but I wasn't content to sit behind a desk. This did not mean that my instinctive desire to teach went away. It just meant that it didn't make sense to me. The tendency prompted me to be a leader with my peers. Unfortunately, since I was heading down a nonconventional path, I might have led others astray. I didn't begin to understand my inner longing to teach until much later in my life. I sense that each one of us is born with a purpose, but uncovering that purpose doesn't always follow with what our life experience is. This has proven to be true in the horse world as well.

It's a western world filled with pickup trucks, dirt roads, chaps, and dusty hats. The men I admire most in this culture are the ones from whom I choose to learn. These men (I believe Ray and Tom included) may not have set out to do horse clinics. They were born to work with horses, not necessarily people; though, as I often quip, "That God, what a kidder."

A horse clinic provides a certain type of education. For some students it's a crash course, for others it is a social network, it can even become somewhat of a religion. Horse clinics are a relatively new game in the greater scope of things, and Ray Hunt offered a unique experiential blend. Ray showed the general public how much potential for learning the horse had. This may have been the platform, but I think what so many people saw was how much could get done in a short amount of time. The caveat was (and is) that just because it took less physically did not mean it took less intellectually. In fact, this was the new induction. Ray encouraged doing less and thinking more. And like so many great virtuosos, he made it look easy. But this shift required the people who attended his clinics to unlearn their old ways and be open to a new way. Ray could work with the horse like a prodigy, but educating people—that was a whole different story.

When a true horseman comes up against a problem in a horse, he can lose sleep trying to figure out a way to reach that horse. There is a dedication to the relationship. It is this relationship between human and horse that is the horseman's craft. The relationship is intimate and thought provoking, and in the best horsemen, it is also spiritual. These horsemen don't only reach deep into the horse; they reach deep into themselves. They are born to do this work, and they wouldn't think of doing anything else.

As a person masters a craft, there is a natural response to share or extend this heightened level of mastery with others. People are drawn to growth. We naturally desire expansion. Teaching becomes part of learning. Ray often mentioned that he got as much out of the clinics as anyone. Our expanded ideas follow us along like rollaway luggage, carrying our insights to our destination. The destination is an evolved, collective mind. The masters of a craft are the guides on this journey, but often they have little or no experience relating to others in this way. I am guessing this may have been one of the greatest challenges of all for my teachers, and now for those who are following their lead.

For so many clinicians, the impervious divide is applying the philosophy they have grown to understand and master with horses to the greater public whom they have come to teach. It is a rare breed of man who can master both nature and the human ego and still find a sense of success within himself. To honor their craft holistically is to bridge the universal gap between mind and heart.

I empathize with these teachers, and I can understand the challenge that lies before them. Relationships of all kinds introduce us to ourselves. When faced with a conflict, we see what is obvious and disagreeable in others. But whether we can recognize it or not, we also feel a strong sense of separation within ourselves. Clinicians have dozens of human egos to respond to each and every week. And I know this can wear them down to the quick. I presume this is an occupational hazard. The students, too, have their own dilemma—between their willingness to improve the relationship they have with the horse and their own fears and doubts of inadequacies. I am no stranger to this cocktail of inspired heart and fearful mind. I have attended clinics most of my adult life. Even now it's as if each one is a first, with all the intensity and complexity of emotions. Learning in a clinic environment offers much more than learning horsemanship. The unknown offers life lessons each time I attend. After nearly thirty years, I still find myself beginning again. These lessons serve their purpose. They grow me. One clinic in particular stands out.

True Grit

It was early spring, and the haul to the ranch clinic took a full day of driving. I felt the enthusiasm that only a new experience can offer. I stepped out of the truck at the ranch and wondered what would come next. I walked over to the round corral and with a big grin shook the clinician's hand. I said, "I'm excited to be here." He said, "Why?" I kind of chuckled, thinking he was kidding, but then I saw he wasn't. So I said, "It's gonna be great!" He said, "We'll see." Well—this was different. But by golly, I had come to learn, and learn I would. Magnus had come along for support, and we had also brought a friend and her horse with us. We made our introductions, settled the horses in their stalls, and took our residence in the little one-room cabin.

The next day introduced me to a brand-new Mary. And, it seemed, one with little tolerance. Within a couple of hours of the first day of class, I was mad as a wet hen. All kinds of things seemed to be frightening my horse Poco. He was shying at every turn. The first time I requested help, I was politely courageous and respectful. Patiently waiting my turn, I said, "Excuse me, my horse seems a bit tight." With scarcely more than a glance over his shoulder, the teacher said, "What do you mean, tight?" I went on to explain that my horse was jumping sideways at every speck of light and rustling oddity. And then I waited. That was it. No more discussion. Comforted by my courage to be vulnerable, I thought, *By all means the teacher will most certainly be watchful. He'll step in when I really need him.* Nope. Then I thought, *I'll get more specific.* Of course, in a very tactful way, I asked, "Is there anything I can do to help him?" Still there was no real guidance other than the old standard, "You might bring his head around."

Just like a horse that sends out a swish of the tail and pins his ears, I had exhausted my warning signals. Finally I screamed out, "Can I get some help here?" My self-preservation had no more patience, and I exploited the right to vocalize it. I had driven four hundred miles to the clinic and felt as if this teacher couldn't care less about me or my horse. This was Poco's second away clinic. The first one had been when he'd bucked me off.

This clinic was five days long and was also geared at working with cattle. The arena was large and inviting to me. It had some obstacles and half-round logs along the walls. There were horses stalled on the other side of the wall, and sunlight streamed in. There were many varied levels of horses and riders. Truthfully I was surprised that Poco was so reactive. I had worked with him all winter, and we had found a lot of success. But this was early spring, and we weren't within the comfort of our familiar environment. At this point Poco and I still had so much to learn about each other. Like every clinic I have ridden in, nothing went as planned. And that's not all bad.

I felt frustrated at the end of the first day. I felt that my horse and I just barely survived. I was surprised that there wasn't more help or guidance from the teacher. I had ridden with this clinician before at a different clinic, but I was on Far Go, who was at his best. This time we were at the clinician's ranch, and my horse and I were far from at our best.

This clinic gave me a perfect place to practice the lessons in life that I have learned. I utilized my lessons in evolving through my pain and allowing new concepts to emerge during times of surrender. These are the times I feel hopeless, unable to change what I am facing. This clinic was one of those times. But if it weren't for the pain, what would show me that I was ineffective? I don't change what feels good. Pain is what motivates change. Pain fuels the need to open myself up and overstep my own perceived limitations.

Breaking down paradigms requires surrendering what we think we know. Acceptance of not knowing is the forerunner to expansion. As I move from level to level in my mind, I begin to see *how* I am seeing. In fact, when I am aware of how I see life, I can more easily see what it is I need to learn. I believe that the shift in how we see things is an important aspect of innovative thinking.

Now, thinking back, I can see the hidden message in the teacher's suggestion to bring the horse's head around. I know now that what I needed was, in fact, to bring my own head around. I needed to see the reality of *what is* rather than what I thought things should be. Neither this world nor this teacher had any intention of rescuing me from my own lessons.

Breaking down paradigms requires surrendering what we think we know. Acceptance of not knowing is the forerunner to expansion.

In clinics I still, even after all these years, show up wanting to be "good enough." I could feel this tendency even through my thin veil of authenticity. It wasn't until my outburst that my true emotions were allowed to boil up through my blood, into my words. At least then, albeit not pretty, it was honest. By the time the first day was done, so was I. I got back to my little cabin and thought that I might as well just go home. Why bother? But I knew that there was no option of bailing out of this clinic. The friend I had brought along was riding in two classes. She had paid double what I had. I was there for the duration. And there were still four days left. Believe it or not, this may have been the hidden blessing. I went to bed stewing, but what came from the proverbial pot the next morning began to "bring my head around."

What do I do with myself when I find I am caught in a world that isn't supporting my point of view or ideals? How do I stay present emotionally in order to gain enough insight to enable my own release from this self-imposed detention? This slow and agonizing mental murder, formed by the opinion that things should be different than they are, holds within it judiciary terms of solitary confinement.

When I find myself wanting to run away, that's the time to pause and look for the clarity that exists within me. The world has always encouraged escape. I want another option. There is a third option that is neither stay nor go, but look, listen, and understand what is buried in the conflict. Acceptance of what is, is my freedom.

The second day of the clinic, I woke early, just as the sun crested the rugged rock cliff in the near distance. The yearling herd was milling around in the corral made of half-round logs. The new foals were running wide open, whinnying for their mothers in a lush green pasture. If ever there was a new day, this was it. And this day was mine to build. I realized I had come for a purpose and set out to understand exactly what that purpose was. I had this day before me, and it sure looked western, with horses, grit, and leather. There I was in the world I had chosen. Now the question remained, What was I going to do with it? I poured my tea and swaddled myself from the crisp morning air and then remembered Ray's important advice to take a fresh start.

So as I pondered my next logical step, I asked myself, *What matters most to me?* I thought about the previous day's events and realized I felt really bad for my horse. I realized I had left him to kind of struggle along, simply because I was in class. I started to realize that I wouldn't have done that at home. His well-being and mine was what mattered. I sure as heck wouldn't have gotten on and ridden him for four hours if he was feeling tight and braced. I wouldn't do it to him, and I wouldn't do it for me. I would have eased off and worked from a success. I would have let go of my agenda. In other words, I would have dealt with what we both were feeling, to the best of my ability.

As I came into the class on the second day, I told my horse, "We've got this, buddy." I walked him around and stayed right at his side as I introduced him to things. We started having some success, and we were both better off. I let go of being "good enough," and he filled right in with his own truth and honesty. I climbed in the saddle after a bit, and there we found more success. Then I stepped down to let him (and me) bask a bit in the glow of overcoming some really big hurdles. If the teacher offered something we were up for, we joined in. If it was a bit much, we backed off. The whole second day was a wonderful experience, and then each day it got better and better.

At one point, things did get a bit exciting. We were riding along on the trail, when a low-hanging branch became wedged in my stirrup, severely poking my horse in the rib. He tightened up as if to buck but then went forward. That caused the stick to jab him even more. We were heading down an incline at a pretty good pace, and the clinician and several others were nearly out of sight. To free us from the branch, I backed Poco up the trail. The stick came free. I was so proud of him for not overreacting. Poco can get really scared really fast, and he had been dealing with his fear all weekend. This challenging experience actually turned out to be one of the most rewarding times of the trip. I got to see Poco look to me for help. Without that unfortunate challenge, I might not have known the depth of what we had built together that week. So you see? The hard stuff was the good stuff. I found a new way of seeing it.

We made it down the mountain and finally caught up with the teacher. There was a group of riders in a draw. The scenery was beautiful—jagged rock backdrops and lush green meadows full of cows and spring calves. I decided to just fall in behind one fella who had come from another ranch to help. He was kind and quiet and, best of all, seemed experienced. I gave myself and

Poco complete permission to be just who we were. This was no time for "trying to be." We moved all the cattle over brush and rock. Poco and I just trailed the group. When we got back, everyone had a turn at sorting a cow out of the herd. I held back and let the others have their fun. I had already gained enough experience for that day. But then our turn came. I just let Poco do his thing his way. Little did I know he would love it. He did a great job, and I put him up for the night. That night I slept like a giant in a hut. I realized that even though the clinic wasn't at all what I'd thought it would be, everything I'd learned was perfect. The whole experience was indeed "Great!"

Surrendering my thoughts of how something is supposed to look allowed me to open my mind and my heart to the opportunity for true and lasting expansion. Horses are my gurus. With forgiveness and patience for my blunderings, they stand at the gate (both literally and metaphorically) and offer me endless opportunities to see them as they are. Horses are good teachers in that they can make stagnation of a learning process seem unbearable. It may be that we hit the ground (or a wall) with a heavy thud only to dust off our hat (or our pride) and reach for a new way to see. Horses offer again and again another try at mastery. Then, if I am willing and open to the message the horse offers, I can find that magical moment of unity. Within this experience of harmony, I sense the oneness of our minds, revealing a presence that transforms us both. My thoughts are released and there is space. This spaciousness makes it possible to receive the gifts my teacher, the horse, is offering. Without the willingness to see such grace, our eyes remain blinded by our own false perceptions.

But often, instead of surrendering when something isn't working, we think we have to fix it. More often than not in my life, the best fix is to first fix my own judgment or perception.

That way I am not trying to make something good out of a bad perception. When I can kick my mind into neutral, I can see a wider perspective. There is a real exciting process in shifting from a negative judgment to a neutral acceptance. I have experienced changes I never thought possible. I have changed my world from the inside out, and with this practice a glimpse at the divine has come.

Surrendering my thoughts of how something is supposed to look allowed me to open my mind and my heart to the opportunity for true and lasting expansion.

Not long after I got back from this clinic, I hosted another clinic at home with my friend and teacher Joe. There was a gal who had planned to attend, though she couldn't get her horse in the trailer. We were on the phone with her and trying to offer support the best we could. At one point Joe said, "Maybe it's best that they can't get the horse in the trailer." I looked at him with questioning eyes. What he said next has absolutely shifted how I see things. He said, "I'm teaching a concept here."

It seems to me that for people to learn to shift their way of doing things, those things often have to go very, very wrong. When we are up against our own thoughts and in a hard spot, we are challenged to change our thoughts. In the end, things turned out well for that gal at our clinic. She brought a different horse, and that horse provided exactly the stability she needed (that day) to learn. Then later, on another day when we had more time and less pressure, we worked with the horse that didn't load in the trailer. This time there was a greater understanding of the importance of how the horse was responding to the request to get in rather than being focused on the outcome. The human began to grasp the concept over the agenda. We shift how we see things, and the things we see change.

When Ray said, "I wish I knew then what I think I know now," he seemed to know that the art of learning was not to believe (too deeply) in what he thought he already knew. I sensed he meant that learning is about chasing a moving target. Knowledge has no ceiling. This might be some of what he gained from his time with Tom Dorrance. I wonder if he found freedom from the confines of his own thinking. I think Tom opened up a brand-new way of seeing things. Then things started changing for the better. It didn't mean there weren't challenges; it meant he saw them as opportunities.

"Don't shoot the guru" means that we see the tough spot as the guru. When we don't try to escape it, change it, or wish something (or someone) is different than it is, we have acceptance. When we have acceptance, our minds are not only free but also open to gain the perfect insight that our world (in that particular moment) is offering us. I am not saying that we stay stuck in the mud. But I am bringing to mind the old proverb "No mud, no lotus." When we practice acceptance, we are also free to find the flower of our consciousness. We break through thought and find a wealth of freedom.

Pain Is the Guru

Ray would answer very directly when asked what to do if a horse bites. His reply was, "If the horse bites you, bear the pain. Next time, don't let him bite you." In other words, take ownership. We can question what happened to better understand the experience. This way the pain actually makes us better. I finally realized, as I lived through the tough times with acceptance, I could begin to appreciate those very things I wish I could have changed. Growth feels good. Learning is what I am here to do, and pain is a masterful teacher. At the very least, my life ceased being so polarized. No longer am I simply bearing the pain. I am utilizing all my experiences for my education.

As I came to understand the value of feeling for my horse (and others), I understood I was learning empathy. "Feel, timing, and balance" was Tom Dorrance's message to us all. It wasn't "Feel it and run away or fight back." It was "feel" to understand, to be in unity. Whether it is for a horse or life, the teaching is offered consistently and poetically through our challenging ex-periences. Spending time trying to eradicate challenge is making plans to shoot the guru.

"Don't shoot the guru" means stay present while in class. It means to know there is a greater understanding that comes to the surface when we are willing to learn. When I discovered this, not only did I stop resisting life and its teachings, but I also actually started craving life. I stopped judging the hard stuff and started unraveling it. When the horse goes to bite, we can be aware and present. I know that my part is to stay far enough away from the horse's teeth so as not to be bitten. The important thing to realize is we don't have to stay away or sell the horse. We can learn what is causing the horse to think he needs to bite. We can heighten our awareness that we have more choices than to blame the horse. We might even find out that we can convince him that he doesn't need to be afraid or defensive. In this way we can help him find better choices. It's not just the horse that learns a better way. In help-ing others, I find different choices for myself too. There are infinite possibilities when we don't fight or flee. Staying in a learning frame of mind, we can inquire into the real question, What can I learn from this? Acceptance doesn't mean that I endure a painful environment, but it doesn't mean I run from it either. Acceptance is all about looking deeper, to inquire into the relationship with the pain.

All or Nothing

While sometimes our response to pain or frustration is to run, it's undeniable that human beings have also formed a habit of annihilation. When life isn't performing the way that we think it should, we tend to want to eradicate things. Our prisons are filled with men and women who are stored like horses on a feed-lot waiting for slaughter. It's a gruesome mind that creates such destruction. At the risk of playing the devil's advocate, one might say, "They know not what they do." They, in this case, are the jailers and the judgers. (Of course the originator of the quote knew this better than anyone.)

In the mind-set of all or nothing, good or bad, stay or go, live or die, we miss the infinite degrees between zero and one.

In the mind-set of all or nothing, good or bad, stay or go, live or die, we miss the infinite degrees between zero and one. We don't learn from those in prison; we judge them. We are quick to the draw. Humans throughout history have destroyed cultures, populations, and even entire species. All because we think "we know," and then we shoot. I see that as insanity. To me I see it as "the mind" that supersedes God. The quip "Who needs God when we have all this control?" comes to mind. It is as if we step in front of the master teacher and say, "Stand down, I've got this."

Yesterday I saw a sticker on a pickup truck that read "Smoke a pack a day." The graphic was of a riflescope, and in the scope was a pack of wolves. It is this all-or-nothing thinking that has created war and has the potential to end the world as we know it. I cannot blame the driver of the truck. He has no choice because he knows no other way. When we shoot first and ask questions later, we lose the potential for learning.

Humans acting out of fear of loss or even potential loss can sometimes complicate matters more. Chaos comes from fear. It is not difficult to see when man has made destruction out of God's perfect creation. Human cultures have always been faced with the primitive sense of kill or be killed. I wish only to convey that education can help us evolve past that primal nature. Education can benefit our world for the long term. The habit of eradication often means we shoot before we have the opportunity to learn what the conditions are telling us. We eradicate rather than educate, and the lessons are lost forever. In this way we are indeed shooting the guru.

"Get to Where You Crave It"

My teacher Joe has a saying that I have adopted for many challenges in my life. He says, "Get to where you crave it." I can even see his face and hear his voice when I repeat these words. What I extracted from that saying through the context of my clinic was that when things aren't going well, there is an opportunity to learn—a teaching opportunity! We can get to where we crave these little spots that show up in our world, in our lives, and in our horses. This is not at all to say that we settle for them but that we realize that we can grow from them.

When Joe was working with me and my horse at our clinic, I felt overwhelmed with frustration. So much so that right in the middle of the class, I rode away in tears. I had worked with my horse Poco for several years. Yet this need to defend and protect just kept rising up in him. I knew that he trusted me and that we had a fantastic relationship, but this habit of escape was big and ingrained. I hated to see him so scared, and quite frankly I would get scared too. At times while riding him, he would jump darn near out of his skin. I wanted Joe's help, yet I felt helpless.

I kept trying to eradicate that little spot. I wanted to change my horse. My mind was stuck in wanting things to be different than they are. I thought that for me and this horse to have peace, things had to change. Joe being my teacher has been one of the most insightful experiences of my education. After Ray and Tom left the physical world behind, I searched for someone who could carry on the work they had spawned in me. Joe has been the only one I have found who is willing to go beyond the surface. He is offering new ways of thinking and seeing "problems" in our horse relationships. Often those ideas are completely the opposite of what the human mind is quick to think. He is indeed teaching a concept, not a technique.

Joe works with us in a brilliant blend of guidance and compassion. As I caved in to my own frustration at this clinic, I rode Poco away from the class and my teacher. I just pointed east, started riding, and thought, *I am not looking back.* With tears rolling, I finally surrendered. I had dealt with this issue for four years, and I was drinking in my lowered opinion of myself. I felt that no matter what I did, I wasn't able to help Poco enough for him to be free of his historic fear. In frustration and humiliation, I was ready to give up.

And then…right there, right in that moment of surrender, I got far enough away from my own thoughts about how my horse "should" act. I accepted exactly who he was in that moment. And with that, I accepted my own fall from grace. I accepted and saw clearly my (not so) little spot. My brilliant teacher said to me, as my tears flowed with abandon, "We may never get rid of that spot, Mary. But we will get everything around it better."

And so I began yet again my journey of the heart, mine and Poco's. I started this new plateau from the very spot I wanted to eradicate. Not only did I accept it, but I also actually became aware enough to feel appreciation for it. I learned love does not eradicate; love is life. Love is trust, and faith, and joy. Right there where we stood is where I wanted to be, and then as it turned out, so did Poco. Poco felt the shift in me, and then with grace that spot naturally shifted, but not before giving me the lesson that changed my life.

When I was riding him a few weeks later, I felt overjoyed and grateful for that little spot. I saw it not as a bad thing but as a beautiful way to grow us both. That spot in both of us held a valuable connection to our freedom. It held what I had been missing, one more piece to the Poco puzzle. And in the months to come, I absorbed even more of what I was learning from Poco. I started to understand that little spot had a life span of its own, and its work had only just begun. I let go of trying to shoot the guru, and now I am eternally grateful for my willingness and that of my horse. Together we learn and together we succeed. And I learned the most important part of learning. I learned to love the guru.

CHAPTER THIRTEEN

Self-Carriage

HERE IN WESTERN OREGON WE HAVE FIR AND MAPLE forests draped with moss and fern. Riding through the woods in late September is a symphony for the senses. The deep green backdrop is accented with fiery yellow leaves and smells of a sweet and earthy tincture. No matter how hot the late summer sun seems, the forest holds its own climate. There is a balance of life supporting life, a natural refuge. The forest is my safe place. It offers, within its simplistic complexity, everlasting flow. It is my microcosm for effective living. The forest doesn't have to brag about its function. The forest is grace, timing, and unity all wrapped up in stunning, alive beauty. All forest elements are interrelated. The trees never say to the moss, "What have you done for me lately?" In a forest one can sense presence and almost hear whispers of wisdom in the wind.

Natural balance is beckoning us through its diabolical contrast, dysfunction. We each possess a threshold for pain and suffering. Humans are naturally drawn to feel pleasure and resist pain. Between those lines is a gradient degree from suffering to ecstasy. And right square in the middle is this little thing called balance. This is the sweet spot. It is flow without waste, health without hype. Balance doesn't have to try or strive to be. It just is. It is creation unified with its offspring, life. This sweet spot is what moves rivers, drops rain, sets the sun, and fills the air. It is beyond man-made technology. It is beyond the ability to intellectualize. It is simply expansion, movement, and evolution. We can't direct it. And when we try, we tend to screw it up. It is easy to see man's mark when he thinks he knows better than nature.

Horses are nature. Man can step in and step on—he can think he knows what the horse should or shouldn't do. But man can never change what is real in the horse. The horse is a horse. And the intimate relationship between man and horse can, and has, taught a fundamental life lesson. Tom and Ray were explaining this lesson for us all. Each of these great teachers was asked to write a book. The books they wrote were small. There just aren't words that definitively describe the beautiful miracle of unity. The titles of their books were good indicators of what the teachings were pointing to: *True Unity* and *Think Harmony with Horses*.

I watched as Ray traveled the world teaching what he himself said could not be taught. He conveyed that he couldn't teach it, but he could make us aware of it. How does one teach harmony? We have to feel it. What we are moving toward is not something that we can make happen. We have to allow it to happen. I learned from Ray that when the horse is ready to do what it is that I am asking of him, I have to know enough to get out of his way and let him do it. This ability to allow things to happen is not common in this "get 'er done" world, though it is the most natural, balanced thing there is. Even the concept of allowing will come when we allow it. We get in the way of God's way—the divine flow, if you will—when we constantly try to make things happen. My deeper understanding of allowing the process led me to this truth and the hidden meaning in the term *self-carriage*.

Before I knew him, my horse Poco had spent half his life in fear. He was five when I bought him. Five years is a long time to develop a way of seeing the world and reacting to it in defense.

To release old habits takes consistent, positive experiences. I desperately want to help Poco understand that he can feel secure. I dig deep into my mind and search for ways to present things so that he can shift his opinion of the world. But I know I can't do it for him. He has to do his part. Knowing this means I set it up and wait and let him find it. Ray taught us to use enough to be effective. He elaborated to be careful not to do too much or too little. This idea has really stayed with me, and it helped me allow Poco his process. It doesn't happen all at once; it happens gradually. In horses and humans we can learn to peel away the layers and habits that fear builds. But it takes time. Developing trust takes our full attention and a desire and willingness to outgrow our past. With consistent, positive influence, trust can begin to shine its light right through the veil of fear.

Relationships grow us, and my relationship with Poco is certainly no exception. I am learning with him. Sometimes he shows me what I need to know, and sometimes I show him a better deal. Then again, sometimes we hold our own. One day, not long ago, I had intended on some one-on-one time with Far Go. But Poco had other plans. He insisted on joining us in the arena. As I led Far Go in from the field, Poco came along. When we got to the arena gate, I just couldn't shut him out. I thought that perhaps he could come in and rest quietly in the center while I rode. Poco had a very different intention. He wanted to do everything Far Go and I did. I realized he enjoys learning now. I have come to understand that the obstacles in the arena have offered Poco confidence by introducing him to a feeling of accomplishment. He overcame his resistance to learning by feeling the exhilaration of success.

As I began to ride Far Go, Poco trotted along behind. I approached a pole on the ground and asked Far Go to straddle it. Poco lined up directly behind us for his turn. Then I went to the teeter bridge, and he followed us there too. I realized through this experience that if I had shut him out at the gate, I might not have had the chance to see how much desire had formed in him. All those obstacles had become what I call the sweet spot. Poco had learned how good it feels to take on a challenge and have a success. This is part of what I learned about self-carriage. Self-carriage is when we have a personal desire to achieve. We are not doing it because someone told us to. We enjoy the feeling of success, and that feeling is what inspires us to learn and grow. We are no longer dependent on other people's opinions to motivate us. We become self-starters. This is what has happened with Poco. He is looking toward the next challenge because he knows the sweet taste of success.

Developing trust takes our full attention and a desire and willingness to outgrow our past.

Self-carriage is not selfish. It is what I found necessary for a successful relationship. I know now that a relationship with a horse or a person doesn't mean that I carry all the burdens. A centered relationship means I feel inspired to be the best I can be because it feels good to live in grace. I wouldn't have it any other way. When I can see life as an opportunity for success, I can see relationships the same way. I learned to read Poco's signals and understand what he needed for support. It felt good to support him. I learned to allow him his process. It was liberating for both of us to know we had a choice and that the other would listen and understand. Poco told me that day that he wanted to be in the arena, and thankfully I adjusted and realized the opportunity in it. Because of that flexibility, I experienced a deeper understanding of where Poco's mind was. Having understanding and empathy in relationships has offered me a new way of seeing others and the world. It was with Poco through self-carriage that I realized one of the most meaningful lessons of all. The lesson of self-carriage and understanding the value of the sweet spot evolved over several years, but it was well worth the wait.

Poco's Lesson

For many years I practiced what I had learned to be self-carriage with my horses. But the problem was I did it only as an exercise; I hadn't yet uncovered the philosophy behind it. I can say now that I honestly had no idea why it was so important—it was just part of my routine. Finally, after five years with Poco, I realized the value as well as the deeper meaning of the practice. Now of course, in hindsight, I wonder how I could have missed it. Poco showed me its benefits, especially for shifting patterns of fear. Self-carriage (it turns out) was how I could present things consistently to my horse. I could present my requests of him and still fulfill his desire for nonresistance. This approach was something Poco could fully grasp and understand. Self-carriage was about giving Poco choices in a soft and simple way. In life, the convergence of resistance and nonresistance can teach us where the sweet spot is. It is the same with horses in the self-carriage exercise. Should my horse stray from the line in the sand (the sweet spot) that I defined through my release of him, *he* then bumps the border. I can let him know with my rein or leg that there is a definite edge there. But for this to be effective, I must be consistent. My response should be in accordance with my horse. He defines how much guidance he needs. I need to be aware, and I need to be early. Being early means alert awareness. This is where Tom's words "Feel, timing, and balance" really come through to enhance my practice. Providing a consistent opening to my horse (so that he can find it) requires my awareness of these three essential elements. Being early means that as my horse bumps the border, he knows it was his action that bumped it. I am not chasing him. The border is consistent, and he knows that line is there.

This alert awareness gives me the timing to offer a complete release when he is on the path of nonresistance, the sweet spot. Soon it takes very little to remind him, and in no time at all, he would rather be there than anywhere. Why would he want to venture away from peace? I can't think of a better example in life of understanding the path of peace. Peace is health, well-being, and freedom. Peace is perfect practice. Soon my horse can walk, trot, or even lope the circle with absolutely no guidance from me. Self-carriage offers unity, the middle ground in duality. And this is a perfect practice to unravel the veil of fear.

Self-carriage has proven to be an invaluable part of my work with Poco. Something very important happens while we are traveling in the sweet spot. Our minds open, our bodies relax, and our union seems effortless. It is not only freedom for him but freedom for me as well. When Poco and I travel in the sweet spot together, there is no past because there is no thought. I say to him, "There you are. I see you." I see him as the beautiful horse that he is. I don't allow his painful past to taint my vision. We have no needs or outcomes that aren't present. We don't have to get further or learn something or be someone other than who we are right here, right now. We are complete. We have acceptance. This is the fundamental message of *Perfect Practice.*

Self-carriage offered Poco a new habit, the habit of feeling free and feeling good. This difference offered us both what we wanted—nonresistance. Self-carriage taught us the value of unity in balance—it offered us both the sweet spot.

Self-carriage has become an excellent metaphor for my life. This is the golden road that offers release from fear. This sweet spot is real, though often overlooked—with our horses and with each other. The release that self-carriage provides is effective in its teaching, especially within fear-based, habituated behaviors. A release of life's pressures feels like freedom. Sometimes we have to bump the borders to understand where our freedom lies. But when I learned that there is a sweet spot, my whole approach to life shifted, and so did my approach to horses.

Shirley's Lesson

I had an early education in knowing the sweet spot as a child. I was every bit as scared as Poco and perhaps even more volatile. My mother must have struggled with me as I have struggled with him. She wanted me to have the peace she knew I was capable of. She would tell me, "Mary Shannon, you can be anything you put your mind to." She had a beautiful mantra she always shared: "I love my children with open arms." She was my safe place to fall. And she loved me through my darkest hours. My mother also held very clear boundaries. She told me I was always welcome home, but I could not just wither away there. Her rule was that I work or go to school, or I don't live at home. These were simple, clear, and consistent requests from which she did not waver.

There were times I bounced hard against her borders. I resisted her rules and ideas of what I should do with my life. I'll bet those were some of her most challenging times. But my wise and beautiful mother knew she was setting a standard in my life. I credit my mother as the reason I have found such success. She didn't have to judge or condemn or deny me my pain. She openly offered a sweet spot and allowed me my process.

My mother never faltered, and our relationship was the most consistent and endearing love I knew in my life. She lived long enough to see me fulfill my dreams. She came here to the canyon before she died and witnessed all I had built. I had my own business, my horses, and my dogs; I had a beautiful home and a sanctuary to live in. She saw how hard I worked and how deeply I loved. She saw me overcome addiction and abusive relationships. She saw me evolve. I know she knew that I was happy.

My mother was named Shirley after the child star Shirley Temple. After she passed on from this lifetime, I inherited enough money to build my riding arena. This single mother of four children had so much reserve in the end, she still provided abundantly for all her children.

The time I spend in my arena is precious. I hold the space as sacred. There is a beautiful garden in memory of Cayenne. In the center fly the prayer flags from my wedding with Magnus. On the walls of the arena are photos I had taken of Ray grinning his infectious grin. And there in the corner is the platform where I sat with Cayenne and read to her on our final night together. Now it is the place I sip my tea. I feel a deep presence in this space. I always feel guided and supported there, and it is where I have the opportunity to share with others what I have learned.

The arena is built from the love that I have known, and it is where so many of my epiphanies take place. This simple horse arena, the space that holds my middle ground, is now named Shirley's Temple. Temples don't always come in the form of a church or a mosque or a grotto. Temples are born from the heart. The space in the center of my being is my constant sweet spot. It is always available and never obstructed. It is ageless and timeless and infinite. Though life and all its difficulties offer the borders I sometimes challenge, now I know, with all that I have learned, how and where to find the middle ground. There is no resistance in the center.

The Beauty and Wisdom in the Self-Care-Age

It was January. The frogs and crickets were singing their introduction for another opening season in this play called life. Spring was early this year. Last year winter lingered long into April. The seasons don't seem to mind if I support their tardiness or not. Nature lives with abandon. In my world the first sign of spring is not the frogs—the first sign is in my horse.

The extremely short winter scarcely gave me time to do my homework. Like the trees and the buds, my horses go a bit dormant in winter. Their life is quiet and refined. My horses spend the long, dark nights munching hay in the barn—their space, their home. There they are cozy, dry, and delightfully occupied by the pleasure of abundant hay. The days are short, and typically, the only real stress is the relentlessly wet ground. The wet ground minimizes movement. Running and bucking are left until spring.

As the season changes, so do the horses. Much like the sky in spring, their coats go from dark to light. Everything in the canyon seems to wake up from a winter's sleep. And with the change is the reminder of all the things I have yet to understand. I have an opportunity in the calm waters of winter to hone my skills. I study my horse throughout the dormant period, but I take my exam in the spring. In the spring I discover what we both learned throughout the winter. Spring is when my horse delivers the next semester's curriculum.

Poco has dark brown eyes that are easy to read. They are like a starless sky on the darkest night. When things are amiss, the black-brown edges turn to white. The contrast indicates a need for my full attention. This characteristic keeps him honest and keeps me aware. Saddling in the spring tends to be a more sensitive issue than in the winter. After several years of seeing Poco shift dramatically from quiet to explosive in the spring, I finally had blood work drawn to understand his chemistry. It was determined that his hormone level was many times higher than an average gelding. This explained so much. With people and with horses, hormones affect emotional responses, and emotional responses affect hormones. It is a prime example of how the body and mind are in tandem. I always try to remember to saddle Poco with care and attentive observance, remembering that a good start is half the finish.

The space in the center of my being is my constant sweet spot. It is always available and never obstructed. It is ageless and timeless and infinite.

Poco's fear is not during the saddling but in the first step. In his past that was when he learned about pain. That first step can hold a lot of meaning for Poco. I have been diligent in my support of his process while offering him a safe place to fall—steadying him if he needs it. I search my soul to help Poco understand that I mean him no harm. I know he understands this when he is loose or even on the end of the lead rope. But then, when I climb into the saddle, something changes. In exploring my own personal journey through the concept of self-care, I realized I, too, feel resistance when I lack trust. There are times I am centered enough with Poco to stay out of the way of his thoughts. But at times my thoughts get in his way. I, too, have history of a painful past with Poco. I was injured twice when he bucked while I was riding him. I finally came to a place through our combined experience where I wondered if we both were having similar thoughts: *Is this the ride that might hurt us?* Were we both bracing against the same fearful thought?

When I step up in the saddle and I lose sight of the present moment, I lose sight of myself and I let my horse down. All my care and well-meaning focus turns my mind into a hologram of what-ifs. I get lost in my own fears, and my horse follows me right in. After all, I am holding the reins. He is taking his cues from me. Why not this one too?

On this particular day, in this particular spring, I awoke to the powerful nature of my own fearful thoughts. I realized I had to change my what-ifs to what *is*. I said out loud to Poco, "You know what? How can you get over your stuff if I won't get over mine?" I was ready for freedom, and that was where I wanted Poco to follow me. After so much "trying to be" and seeking to find the answers, I was willing to be right where I was. I was finally willing to be present.

From that moment, there was nothing to fix. I surrendered my thoughts. If Poco needed support, I helped; otherwise, I left him to do his work. This mirror shines right into my human relationships too. I tried to fix things that truthfully weren't mine to fix. I couldn't fix my sister's demise from alcohol or my beloved Cayenne's terminal illness. I had to live life on life's terms. Those kinds of life situations do just that: they wake us up when we are willing to accept what is.

Acceptance in no way means I don't ride; it means I don't try to control things that haven't even happened. I take care of my part in this moment and leave the rest up to the rest. That is how I tied self-carriage together with self-care-age.

I see self-carriage as a necessary lesson for our world. As I realized that self-care was not selfish, I also began to see that when I heal myself the world around me shifts too. I healed the pain and fear that I acquired early in my life, and then I began to see the world differently. I was free to see love. I was also free to understand that aggression comes from fear. I could see that anger was a result of a sense of loss. I began to understand things on a deeper level. I could empathize rather than rationalize. But I couldn't have done this until I began to heal myself. Now I can see that my life is but a microcosm of the world. I am not different from anyone else. I just became aware of the sweet spot by looking deeply into my pain. I let the pain be the border. I decided I don't want all this resistance in my life. It simply just doesn't feel good. I came of age—you might say, self-care-age. I sense the world is bridging the same transition.

When my own self-care was combined with my teaching tool (the exercise of self-carriage), I found a way for my horse and me to transform our world. I mean this in the truest sense. When we change how we see the world, the world changes. I stopped seeing Poco as broken and started to empathize with his fear. His fear is real to him. I wasn't going to fix it, but I could show him he was capable. I showed him confidence by offering new things to learn, and he succeeded. He became brave. Sure, fear showed up. But when it did, I was there to support him, not condemn him. Poco saw me as an ally. And this is how we developed what is, to me, the most important element of riding—our relationship.

How we see others and how we see our world will make a difference in how we see our lives. I have touched on this concept throughout this book. The power of perception could be more accurately called the power of persuasion. We hold much more power in our own minds than we could ever implement through force or control. I have mentioned that control is temporary and dependent. It requires manipulation of outside forces, and that is certainly a false security. Self-care-age is when we take ownership for our part in the process. It is the most selfless thing we can do.

Fear's Lessons

Early on in my life and in my horsemanship, I was afraid to make mistakes. I began to recognize the malady of misdirected desire. The desire to have unity conflicted with feeling compelled to control the outcome. The two tendencies were opposing counterparts. For decades I experienced my life through micromanaging all the variables—my jobs, my relationships, my education, and even the most sacred element of my life, my relationship with horses.

The power of perception could be more accurately called the power of persuasion. We hold much more power in our own minds than we could ever implement through force or control.

The need to control things is born from fear, and fear comes from lack of understanding. There is only one place on the planet where we are free to see perfectly, and that is deep within ourselves. All else is perception. Perception is not truth and falls prey to debate. Even those in my life who know me best still can't know me from my own depths. My husband often says he sees me as strong and independent. But I can still feel scared and weak like everyone else. He is not wrong to make assumptions based on what he sees, but the ability to communicate authentically helps us have a real and meaningful relationship. No one can completely know another, even if we think we know that person well. Controlling our world based on assumptions can be a disappointing approach to life. But understanding another with empathy and listening in order to understand can build a lasting bond. When I stopped trying to control my world and my horse, I opened myself to learning what my horse and the world had to teach me.

The horse and life don't need my judgment; they need my attention. They are my teachers. I am here to learn. In order to fully understand what is outside of me, it's best to understand what's going on inside. I can come to know the witness, the perceiver, the watcher and understand my deepest self. I can observe how I see things. It can be difficult to do that if I am busy fixing everyone and everything else around me.

Self-care is returning to that place inside me where I see most accurately. This is a place of presence and alert awareness. I don't forget the little self—the mind-occupied self with all its thoughts, opinions, and judgments. I just don't see it as who I am. I see it for what it is—a sprout from the hard-packed soil of my tradition. Most of my outdated opinions didn't even come from me. I adopted them from what someone else told me was true. Or sometimes my judgments came from my opinions of someone else's opinion. But none of this is true; it all comes from perception.

The little self is the sum total of my experiences plus how I reacted to those experiences. The little self is the one who remembers hitting the ground hard when the horse shied. She is the one who is afraid of the outcome. That little insecure self has a need for control, and that need comes from fear. Fear is a perception, and rarely is it true.

There is a deep peace that returns to the mind when the frightened child is not running the household. I learned to trust, and perhaps I will eventually unlearn fear. I can let the little self (who is deathly afraid) find solace and shelter in simple peace of mind. And just like the little light that Tom and Ray brought to humanity through the horse, I, too, can shine that light on myself. All that *is* flourishes with such understanding.

Ray and Tom offered a look into how unity can develop from completely opposing counterparts. The horse-human relationship is a living example of finding the middle ground between one identity and another. It is a prime example because it is intensely dualistic by nature.

Horses are large enough to make it very worthwhile for the human to be effective. They have all the sheer force required to show us that our life can depend on bridging the mental gap that separates us. Like many other types of conflicting circumstances, true effectiveness in horsemanship highly depends on developing unity. The horse is a masterful teacher of unity when we allow it. Horses are spiritual enough to hold the presence of forgiveness for the world in which they live—and powerful enough to show us the value in harmony.

The horse's divine quality is present as a blend of power and peace. This beautiful, natural characteristic creates a perfect experience for our thought-driven mind to integrate with our love-based heart. This integration is the evolved human, a human who can use the intellect as a tool, not as the means to an end, a human whose only real purpose is peace.

The willingness to open to a new way of seeing is like coming full circle around a spiral. Each pass brings us a bit closer to the center. To see the horse (or life) anew with each completed phase means being willing to let go of outdated beliefs. Those old beliefs are necessary for a time, but they are a transient element of the evolution of the mind. My old models brought me to this place in my life, but now it's time for me to move on.

Shedding identity after identity feels like a death of sorts. It is a process known as *dying to self*. Allowing my old ways to die off so new ways can emerge takes a bit of getting used to. The transition has become a bit smoother with time. But still there is a twinge of grief for the old, outdated self. Letting her go is like finally throwing out that favorite pair of worn-out boots that have been repaired one too many times. It's time to let them go and break in a new pair. And so it is with peeling the layers of my beliefs. Once the transition is complete, it feels excitingly wonderful, though the path leading up to that point is best served by a patient and compassionate heart.

Horses are spiritual enough to hold the presence of forgiveness for the world in which they live—and powerful enough to show us the value in harmony.

My friend Joe tells how he really opened up to a greater understanding of what's effective with horses when he let go of being right. This is brilliance in education, though it is a highly uncommon attribute of the human psyche. Humans pride themselves on being right, on being the intelligent species. And if someone is a paid professional, that person makes a living by being right. These great teachers, Ray, Tom, and Joe, are exceptional because they encourage being open to making mistakes. Making mistakes identifies what we need to learn.

Can you do less? I hear Ray's voice in these words. Of course, like countless other people within his reach, I thought I was doing less! But then of course I know there is always so much more to learn, so much more to understand, so much more "less." It is a cycle. These are the moments when the concepts of what I thought I knew come to an end and it's time to move on. The years of inquiry and unpacking of thoughts combine with yet another level of understanding, and I become open and willing to receive the next level of lessons. The cycle of learning begins again, and I ask myself, *Is that what Ray meant?* It's not likely that I will ever stop asking that question. It is what keeps me reaching for my own answers.

Of course Ray and Tom have moved beyond their bodies, so it is impossible to answer that question. But before they took their leave, they planted fields of plenty in the minds of many. Echoes of thought-provoking one-liners such as Tom's wise words "Observe, remember, and compare" and the deeper meaning of the phrase "It all depends" fill the minds of trail riders and cowboys alike.

Those of us with inquiry as our hidden habit quenched our thirst from the well of deeper knowledge. New thoughts and understandings were born from these one-line statements. We disciples of this way of seeing and relating to our horses are still pondering unanswered questions. And that is exactly the point. The one-word sentence from Ray—"Think"—reminds us that thinking is exactly what they wanted us to do.

Some students want a teacher to tell them what to do. They would much rather follow instructions than take initiative. We are students because we believe that something (or someone) outside of us has the answers we seek. Dedicated students will gladly invest time, money, and focused attention in the people they believe in. I found, however, that this is only half the equation. I began to recognize that my pie-in-the-sky way of looking at my teacher was holding me back. I was getting stuck somewhere in my mind.

I realized I was seeing myself as "less than." This fear of inadequacy really began to taint my open mind. It not only didn't feel good, but it also certainly wasn't harmony. I realized, yet again, that I was trying to force something. I was forcing my learning. The comparing mind was stepping in front of my natural ability to grow and learn. This was a big piece of the puzzle. This little spot of unworthiness had taken hold, and it grew before I even knew it was there.

I felt that I was moving forward in my learning. But I also knew there was something very important to grasp in this sensation of inadequacy. It felt like I was leaning on a curtain. There was nothing solid there. As I looked into myself, I saw other gaps in my learning stemming from the same taproot. The problem with beliefs is the burden of proof. When we are willing and open to understanding, we don't have to prove anything. It's all about experiment, and trial and error. Mistakes happen, and we learn from them. The purpose and the desire for understanding take precedence over the need to prove something is right.

No matter how much success I experienced, I was inwardly plagued by this burden of proof. It followed me like a dark shadow. I wanted to satisfy this lack, but the problem was that I was seeing the lack, not that I was lacking. This is another fine, cavernous line. There was no self-care, only self-judgment. I finally understood that there was nothing to prove. I was all right already. I couldn't care for a self that I was hell-bent on changing. I had to learn to love her at the same time I was guiding her forward. And this is exactly what I had to learn to do with my horse as well.

The longing for learning had shifted unconsciously into wanting to be right and being afraid of making mistakes. I was cloaked in a veil of passion for my craft. I mistakenly saw this burning desire as ambition. But I was blinded by enthusiasm. I never saw it coming. That dark shadow finally tripped me up enough times that I reached for something different. I began to ask questions. That's where it shifted. My desire for understanding rose back to the surface, and I looked to the source of the dysfunction. I realized I had gone from wanting what was best to seeking approval. Thankfully once I recognized this, I was hot on the trail to turn it back around. This is what had to happen before what I wanted to have happen happened. The good news is that I am in good company on this quest for deeper understanding. And now I can look at my mistakes with a smile.

The exercise I practiced, called self-carriage, offered a deeper understanding of unity with my horse. I heard Ray speak of the epiphany when he said that we will never be able to believe how little it takes and how much we'll get back from our horses. I felt this idea well up inside of me as I rode Poco one evening. All these years and finally in one divine moment it came streaming into me. There I was, offering nothing. No thing, no resistance, just openness to Poco. Of course being on his back is still a physical burden, though what I speak of is more about the mind. In our minds I could sense the same intention. I stopped my thoughts from blocking his. And this was indeed so much less! It was freedom and acceptance. Poco found freedom because that is in his nature. He wanted nonresistance as much as I did—perhaps even more.

I had been getting in his way. I thought I knew what he needed, but I couldn't have known. My knowing was a perception, and that perception was false. There in Shirley's Temple, on one fine spring evening, I felt unity through freedom. This open-ended, unified rhythm of Poco and me in the sweet spot was the longing in my soul, echoed back to me from my horse. My horse and I were of one mind. It wasn't about riding any longer. I had been given the opportunity to *be* the sweet spot, to be a place of nonresistance. It no longer mattered to me what task we were doing. We could experience unity anywhere, in any cadence, thought, or feel. The important concept that I had a glimpse of was that there was no force. But this did not mean we

were passive. It meant mutual respect. It meant understanding
life is a circle. Life is love. Not physical love or intellectual love,
but love as in nonresistance. This is not about horses. This is
horses teaching about life. Think Harmony and True Unity are
what perfect practice means to me.

---

*I had been given the opportunity to be the sweet spot, to be a
place of nonresistance.*

I have attempted to describe my own personal journey here,
through my stories and my tales. These are my life experiences.
As Carolyn Hunt said to me as I began the writing of this book,
"Mary, this is your story. It is your interpretation of Ray's words."
It is so important to me to remember that what is truth is a relative term. In this case, what I heard Ray say had meaning to
me only after it was filtered through my interpretation. No one
could truly know Ray's meaning, and (frankly) I don't think he
wanted us to. Just as he said of the horses, "I want them to do my
thing their way." I think he also wanted us to do his thing our way.

I've shared my life in these pages. This life is the simple, ele-
gant, messy, intelligent, rebellious, caring, fiery, vulnerable, deep,
curious, authentic and refuting, loving and contesting expression of my soul. That is how life is developed and expressed.
This particular life is a peculiar story called Mary—a miniscule,
distinct illustration of God. There is only one story like mine.
When I join my divine purpose with that of a horse, this, too,
becomes unique and the bonded connection irreplaceable. For
me, recognizing the intense significance of this bond was just
the beginning of realizing unity in all life.

Acknowledgments

FIRST I WISH TO ACKNOWLEDGE TWO OF THE MOST important people in my life, my husband, Magnus Bergroth, and my best friend, Ann Reichle. Without their constant encouragement, support, and exceptional editing skills, this book may not have been completed. For four years they have nurtured my creative process. They have been patient listeners, as well as fair and honest critics. They were always available when I needed advice and compassion. Thank you, Magnus and Ann. This is our book.

These stories and the messages within would not have been possible without the dedication of the master teachers Ray Hunt, Tom Dorrance, and Joe Wolter. A common thread of perfect practice was evident to me in each one of these men, though apparent in very different ways. Thank you.

I also want to acknowledge with heartfelt appreciation the wives of these three great men, Carolyn Hunt, Margaret Dorrance, and Jimmie Wolter. I know that each of these fine women have had the difficult job of supporting behind the scenes, and their dedication and love fortifies all the teachings.

I wish to acknowledge added appreciation to Carolyn Hunt for the ongoing support over the many years that it took to write this book. I couldn't have realized how that support would become a transformative blessing. When I first started writing this book, I set the intention to illustrate how Ray taught life lessons to me through the horse. It was imperative that I conveyed Ray's teachings authentically. Your approval, Carolyn, was vital, but then I received so much more. You consistently reminded me this is my story, not Ray's. From our first correspondence to the last, you encouraged me to write my story. To a great degree, the quality of my book is because of this encouragement. Thank you, Carolyn.

Thank you to the late Margaret Dorrance. I could not have imagined that your approval of this manuscript would come in the final week of your life. It was a rare and ultimate blessing to have had a glimpse into your perspective of Tom's wisdom, as well as your beautiful, spunky humor. Thank you, Margaret. I also wish to extend my sincere appreciation to Steve Dorrance for carrying out the task of formally granting me permission to use all the quotes by Tom Dorrance mentioned in these pages.

About the Author

MARY CORNING HAS NAVIGATED HER WAY THROUGH addiction and codependency. She has felt rejection and abandonment. She has suffered and pondered the depth of grief and loss. She watched as dementia transformed the mind of a loved one. She has received the shocking news of suicide. You might say her credentials are an advanced education in life. However, pain alone cannot offer wisdom. Mary had to be willing to look deeply into these experiences. She lived through them with a clear and conscious mind, and her heart prevailed. These are the experiences that brought her to the wisdom, but her willingness offered the understanding for applying it to life.

Mary's education in life expanded when she met her teacher Ray Hunt. Ray taught her about horses, and horses in turn taught her about herself. This education required a great investment. She became completely dedicated to finding her purpose. Ray Hunt and the philosophy he taught seemed to fit her curriculum perfectly. That was thirty years ago, and she is still in class. A philosophical approach to horses or to life is not an education that ends with a degree. In fact, it never ends. And that is the beauty of it. Perfect practice doesn't mean we reach perfection—it means we never settle for less.

Mary lives in the Willamette Valley of Oregon on twenty acres of land at the foothills of the Coast Range. She is blissfully married to her husband, Magnus, who is her life's perfect partner. She has a best friend who vitalizes her whole heart with an unwavering friendship. Mary is passionately involved with her horses and dedicated to her work with people. She loves life, and her home includes two wonderful stepsons who have given her the gift of a front-row seat into youthful expression. Her constant companions and confidants are her dogs and cats. When she is not writing, working, or enjoying her home life, her favorite pastime is horse camping in one of western Oregon's many beautiful forests.

About the Speaker

A S A SUCCESSFUL MENTOR, WRITER, LIFE CONSULTANT, and equine behaviorist, Mary Corning shows her audiences that they can shift their perspective and change their world.

As a speaker, Mary Corning introduces us to ourselves in a way that feels familiar and comforting. The philosophy is not complicated. It is indeed very simple. When we reunite with our own authenticity, we gain acceptance for ourselves and others. Regardless of profession, family status, age, or socioeconomic level, the practice of acceptance offers an opportunity for deeper understanding. Our perspective is broadened and literally shifts how we see the world. This deeper understanding offers us the wisdom to make positive choices.

Mary shares this philosophy of living an authentic and transparent life through many topics. These are the components for living the life we are born to live, and they offer us freedom within it.

+ Practicing Acceptance for Real and Lasting Change
+ Improving Difficult Relationships and Expanding Positive Ones
+ Shifting Fear to Curiosity to Identify Positive Choices when Fear Is Present
+ Recognizing the Early Signals of Defensiveness within Ourselves and Others

+ Defining the "Illogical Logicals": Using the Psychological, Biological, and Sociological Influences of the Human Condition as Tools, Not as an Identity
+ Releasing the Heavy Load of Obligation and Creating Inspired Dedication

Through keynote addresses, small-group talks, workshops, conferences, and retreat settings, Mary speaks to:

+ Personal enrichment groups
+ Women's, men's, couples', and youth groups
+ Recovery groups
+ Grief support groups
+ Civic groups
+ Business professionals
+ Team builders

To learn more, to book Mary for your group or conference, or to hear what others share about their experiences in Mary's audience, go to www.MaryCorning.com.

CPSIA information can be obtained
at www.ICGtesting.com
Printed in the USA
BVHW041158021121
620559BV00014B/164